D1403552

DO YOU HAVE WHO IT TAKES?

DO YOU HAVE WHO IT TAKES?

MANAGING TALENT RISK IN A HIGH-STAKES TECHNICAL WORKFORCE

STEVE TRAUTMAN

GREENLEAF
BOOK GROUP PRESS

ALSO BY STEVE TRAUTMAN

Teach What You Know:
A Practical Leader's Guide to Knowledge Transfer Using Peer Mentoring

The Executive Guide to High-Impact Talent Management

This publication is designed to provide accurate and authoritative information in regard to the subject matter covered. It is sold with the understanding that the publisher and author are not engaged in rendering professional services. If expert advice and/or assistance is required, the services of a competent professional should be sought.

Published by Greenleaf Book Group Press
Austin, Texas
www.gbgpress.com

Copyright ©2017 The Steve Trautman Co.

All rights reserved.

No part of this book may be reproduced, stored in a retrieval system, or transmitted by any means, electronic, mechanical, photocopying, recording, or otherwise, without written permission from the copyright holder.

Distributed by Greenleaf Book Group

For ordering information or special discounts for bulk purchases, please contact Greenleaf Book Group at PO Box 91869, Austin, TX 78709, 512.891.6100.

Design and composition by Greenleaf Book Group and Kim Lance
Cover design by Greenleaf Book Group and Kim Lance
Cover images: © Marina R; © notbad. Used under license from Shutterstock.com.
© Bannosuke/iStock Collection/Thinkstock

Cataloging-in-Publication data is available.

Print ISBN: 978-1-62634-430-3

eBook ISBN: 978-1-62634-431-0

Part of the Tree Neutral® program, which offsets the number of trees consumed in the production and printing of this book by taking proactive steps, such as planting trees in direct proportion to the number of trees used: www.treeneutral.com

TreeNeutral

Printed in the United States of America on acid-free paper

17 18 19 20 21 22   10 9 8 7 6 5 4 3 2 1

First Edition

To Sonja Gustafson and the fun, creative,

and courageous STC team, working every day to change

the world by bringing these ideas to light.

Contents

The Challenge and Promise of Managing Your Talent Risk

I ONCE HEARD THE CHIEF RISK OFFICER FOR A MAJOR INTERNATIONAL insurance company describe the president of her region as the "chief risk taker." Depending on your viewpoint, that could sound like a pejorative or a compliment. When you think of chief risk taker, do you picture a daredevil dressed like Elvis preparing to ride his motorcycle up a ramp and over a row of buses? Or do you picture a bespectacled accountant with a green visor, poring over the ledger and counting pennies? I'm guessing more the former than the latter, and that makes sense.

"Bold leadership" is at the top of the list of characteristics we expect of our senior executives, and no one ever made a movie about a boss who played it safe. Still, do you really want Elvis-on-a-motor-cycle out front in your company? Of course not. But when it comes to managing the people component of business, that is sometimes what it seems like. Executives have had to settle for setting strategy, hir-ing "good people," and hoping the risk of failure isn't too great. They are missing an important perspective that can guide them to more predictable success. *We have to gather data and make a plan to help Elvis land that bike safely on the other side.*

To be clear, I don't think anyone sets out to be careless when it comes to managing talent risk. It is just that they do not know how to do it—or even realize that it can be done at all. This is especially true when the talent risk involves technical workers like scientists, engineers, analysts, artists, mechanics, operators, and project managers. Assessing and mitigating the risk of having enough of these unique technical skills required to execute your strategy seems like a non-starter. The likelihood of having these skills in place should be driven by more than luck and a current organizational chart.

> Successfully managing talent risk involves no sprinkling of pixie dust. It is actually a collection of common sense ideas that, when knit together, may seem magical but are really just straightforward and actionable practices that can happen at all levels of an organization."

In this book, I want to introduce a radical—even revolutionary—but *entirely practical* new way to think about, talk about, and solve this problem. It will help you better control the continuum between daredevil and bean counter on talent with a quick, clear, and simple methodology. You can do it with structured conversations founded in meaningful data on the people who create your competitive advantage.

Sound too utopian? Successfully managing talent risk involves no sprinkling of pixie dust. It is actually a collection of common sense ideas that, when knit together, may seem magical but are really just straightforward and actionable practices that can happen at all levels of an organization.

TALENT RISK IS LIKE NO OTHER RISK. OR, IS IT?

We already assess and manage many types of business risk day to day, including legal, operational, financial, and insurance. You would never dream of just going with your gut when it's a matter of legal risk or worker safety. No boardroom would settle for "I have a feeling our production capacity can meet the anticipated demand." And even though in-house risk managers and out-of-house vendors (lawyers, insurance brokers) may shoulder the heavy lifting, nearly every line executive has at least a basic understanding of how to address common types of business risk and where to go for help. Well, except for one risk area. Though you and your organization manage risk diligently in other business areas, no one methodically manages technical talent risk.

I want to introduce a new framework and lexicon for managing your technical talent risk. Together, we can learn to answer talent risk questions like—

- If you inherit a team, department, division, or whole company, how do you quickly get your head wrapped around the critical talent and their function?

- What does it cost in time and money to develop or replace experts with unique technical knowledge—*and what can go wrong in the meantime?*

- If you pull expert staff from an existing critical role to take on next-generation projects, how do you make sure the existing function doesn't implode?

- If you purchase a company because of their technical expertise, how do you retain the right experts? How do you keep them productive and happy so they stay after the deal closes?

- If you level workloads between teams, how can you identify unintended consequences and reduce their impact?

- If you reduce head count through attrition or reduction in force, how do you know if enough of the right people will still be on the team?

- If you outsource a function to a third-party vendor, how do you know their job performance will meet your company standards?

- How long will it take to staff a new strategy, and what is the impact on the existing work?

- How can you measure if every employee "gets" your new strategy and can make thoughtful decisions as they execute it?

THE RELEVANT DATA AND THE "SECRET SAUCE"

Although executing any business plan obviously involves people, there is this myth that you can't manage the "people part" of change with data, facts, and the same degree of clarity that you apply to other types of business risks. Some people think there is no real way to glean—much less use—*clear, measurable,* and *detailed* data on talent risk. They think you can't quantify the risk associated with technical talent in dollars and put a timetable to the risk's reduction. They think you can't articulate the risk in a spreadsheet.

New methodologies and recent tools from the field of talent risk management prove these notions are wrong. Not only is managing talent risk with data *possible,* it can also be done with a level of control such that you can punch up or dial back key variables relatively quickly to respond to different business needs. I will show you that you can be aligned globally with fellow stakeholders (crossing boundaries of location, reporting structure, generation, culture, and language) so that when you express concerns over your talent risk profile (or

> " The framework begins with relevant and accessible technical talent data. The data is more than just demographics, engagement numbers, and job ladders. It needs to include details. You need to know what they *do* for you—down to the keystroke, the turn of a wrench, the drop from a pipette, or the invention of a big idea."

theirs), you'll be able to collaborate efficiently to solve the problem. I'll show a rich framework for how to talk within your team, among your peers, and up and down your global leadership chain, as well as between business units and across the boardroom table. The framework begins with relevant and accessible technical talent data. The data is more than just demographics, engagement numbers, and job ladders. It needs to include details. You need to know what they *do* for you—down to the keystroke, the turn of a wrench, the drop from a pipette, or the invention of a big idea.

We sometimes call this their "secret sauce."

Once you have that data, it needs to be available at the right level at the right time. It needs to work like Google Earth. Remember your first time using that app? You opened it and you were looking at the world. Then, you found that a few simple clicks let you zoom in on your continent, then your country, state, and city. A few more clicks took you to your neighborhood. Then you were looking at the street corner in front of your home and your own front door. Your talent risk data needs to zoom in and out the same way—from the global organization down to an individual worker on a team and then to the unique work he or she does for you every day.

For your talent risk data to be useful, the process to gather it and the framework to assess it can't be too arduous. We have to get at this data quickly and keep it up to date without adding a fleet of statisticians.

Sound too good to be true? First, let me say that this is not just theory. The ideas in this book have come about through practical, boots-on-the-ground work with scientists, engineers, developers, analysts, and other technical experts (starting with thousands at Microsoft in the early 1990s) in more than twenty-five countries. They have been validated both by observable results in the field and through ongoing research.

ARE WE SPEAKING THE SAME LANGUAGE? TALENT RISK DEFINED

An online video game company planned to move an entire game franchise from their offices in San Francisco to Bangalore. Roughly one hundred roles—designers, artists, project managers, engineers, testers, and leadership—would need to be set up in India in a matter of months. The new team in Bangalore would shepherd the company's highly profitable game going forward, while the San Francisco team would focus on the next big idea. Before this could happen, the San Francisco team needed to replicate their skill set in the team in India. Once hired, the new team would sit with their American counterparts until the US-based employees were peeled off for new "strategic" projects.

The problem was that while the US-based team members were great coders and gamers, they had no idea how to transfer their knowledge, beyond providing months of job shadowing. Plus, the team in India was being hired by recruiters who only had job titles and little else to go on. Most of the new team members would be hired on a Monday in Bangalore and then fly to San Francisco on that Friday for three to four months to sink or swim. What could possibly go wrong?

This is talent risk.

Talent Risk can be defined as the potential for gaps between your current *technical/professional capacity*—the people who currently perform critical tasks within your organization—and your projected resource demands for the next three to thirty-six months. These gaps are your talent risk. The gaps are more than just the lack of people. It is also the lack of backups that can result in critical single points of failure in your workforce. Every organization has talent risk. What matters is if your organization knows where the high risks lie and what you are doing to reduce your "unacceptable," "high priority," or "critical" risk effectively.

Talent Risk Management (TRM) is the process of *assessing* your current technical/professional capacity compared to the expected three- to thirty-six-month demand, *aligning* your organization around which risks are a priority, and then *taking mitigating action* to reduce the highest risk. It uses detailed, targeted data to monitor your talent risk profile and tune the makeup and readiness of your team. It means you can say with justifiable confidence that you have enough of the right technical/professional people with the right skill sets in the right place at the right time to stay productive, innovative, and competitive. And it means you know the financial impact of your risk at all times.

Firms that approach TRM through the lens of their strategic workforce planning initiatives, like KPMG International and Deloitte, have put forth their own definitions of talent risk management. KPMG International defines TRM simply as "having the right people in place at the right time to drive current and future business growth."[1]

Talent risk management has similarities to strategic workforce planning, but it is not the same. Talent risk management has a greater emphasis on measuring technical/professional capacity, identifying and aligning organizations around talent risk priorities, and taking measurable action to mitigate those risks.

SOME COMMON BUSINESS CHALLENGES ROOTED IN TALENT RISK

No matter how we define the field of talent risk management, we know that business leaders make big decisions every day without truly understanding their risk. Imagine the stronger outcomes if the following organizations could tap into a clear and simple way to think about talent risk.

- The board of directors for a major corporation knows that investors and financial analysts are focusing more and more on talent and human capital because it can account for up to 15 percent of valuations.[2] Historically, boards rely on succession planning

1   "Time for a More Holistic Approach to Talent Risk: Global Risk Survey Calls for a New Take on Talent Management," KPMG International, November 2013.
2   "Focus on Talent Intensifies for Corporate Boards and Senior Executives," *Nasdaq GlobeNewswire*, October 15, 2013.

for top-tier leaders to guard against talent risks. However, for companies to experience sustained growth and profitability in a highly connected world, boards need to look beyond their top tier when looking at talent. They need a multigenerational, multiethnic, and multiskilled workforce. *How will the board hold management accountable for making sure that talent at all levels never becomes a barrier to the execution of their strategy?*

- A global contractor in oil and gas needed eighty new Project Managers (PMs) to handle multibillion-euro projects around the world. Due to a combination of growth and retirements, the corporation needed these highly specialized PMs to be ready to run megaprojects within three years instead of the seven years it had typically taken in the past. Billions in client contracts hinged on providing qualified PMs in the set timeframe. *How will management grow the talent it needs, consistent with a global standard, in time to meet the demands of its clients?*

- The same contractor faced the challenge of cross-cultural and cross-generational talent development. As a multinational corporation, they might have an Italian expert with white hair teaching a Malaysian millennial with pink hair and tattoos. Or a forty-year veteran might need to learn from someone young enough to be his grandchild. Talk about bridging a gap. *How will management help its knowledgeable employees cross the cultural and generational gaps to work with and develop their talents?*

- Two longtime rival companies announced to the press that they would merge their firms. These two companies had technology that, when joined, could dominate their sector. Employees from both companies groaned as they read the details online. They knew they were in for one to two years of craziness as the two former enemy organizations fought for dominant roles in the new "blended" family. Almost immediately, employees' phones began to ring with calls from headhunters eager to lure them away from this mess. *How will leaders manage talent risk during a merger to ensure that the best technical professionals see a future for themselves in the new organization and stay so they can be part of it? Once the merger is complete, how will management get everyone back to work, with clear job roles and expectations, within days or weeks rather than months or years?*

- A medical devices manufacturer was running three shifts to keep up with demand for their lifesaving product. The assembly required more than bolting components together. It was so specialized that the technicians had to be taught how much pressure to exert with their fingertips to get just the right tension. One false move and hours' worth of painstaking work would become scrap. New employees had over twenty hours of formal training and had access to carefully documented protocols. But they also always came in on the night shift because that was where all the low-seniority people started. Sure, they could learn from a few longtime employees who worked nights, but the deep experts who truly understood the process worked days. The product was continually plagued with consistency and quality problems. *How will management ensure a standard is clear across multiple teams? Who exactly sets the standard, and who is supposed to follow it? Once the standard is clear, how will management ensure that every new hire can perform to that standard before they make expensive or even life-threatening mistakes?*

All these examples represent real businesses that eventually turned to talent risk management for a solution to their business challenges. Whether I'm talking to executives in industries like IT and software, finance, energy, big pharma and biomed, transportation, or manufacturing, I hear the same basic sentiment: "Of course we know we have these talent problems, but we don't know how to solve them."

Dan Roberts, president of Ouellette & Associates (O&A)—a Boston-area IT professional development and consulting firm to Fortune 500s—agrees. He recently told me, "I work closely with CIOs, CTOs, and large technical organizations. These people don't think there's anything out there to help them when it comes to talent risk, but they're under intense pressure every day. Today's CIO is trying to transform culture. They're trying to change how IT does business by moving up the IT maturity curve—from simply supplying services to being an innovative anticipator with a seat at the strategy table. And the company is pressuring the CIO, saying, 'We need more from you. We need it faster from you. We need it different from you.' Their world and technologies are changing so fast. And it keeps coming back to *talent*. Talent, talent, talent. The war for talent is *not* a cliché in IT."

Multiple research studies support what Dan is seeing. A reported 41 percent of organizations have problems retaining critical-skill employees, and the percentages have been trending upward the last four years:[3] Businesses are at risk of losing top talent, and it's not because of an aging workforce. Forty-four percent of millennials say that if given the choice, they expect to leave their current employers in the next two years. That figure increases to 66 percent when the time frame is extended to 2020.[4] While we know managing risk associated with our top technical talent is a pressing issue, an astonishing 85 percent of organizations report that their talent management programs and policies need an overhaul.[5]

> **"While we know managing risk associated with our top technical talent is a pressing issue, an astonishing 85 percent of organizations report that their talent management programs and policies need an overhaul."**

---

3 "The Targeted Employee Value Proposition: Drive Higher Performance Through Key Talent and Differentiated Rewards," 2013–2014 Talent Management and Rewards Study, North America, Willis Towers Watson, December 2013.
4 "The 2016 Deloitte Millennial Survey: Winning Over the Next Generation of Leaders," Deloitte Touche Tohmatsu Limited, January 2016.
5 "Future-Proofing HR: Bridging the Gap between Employers and Employees," 2016 Global Talent Trends Study, Mercer LLC, April 2016.

FROM KNOWLEDGE TRANSFER TO MANAGING TALENT RISK

Most people know me from my work in *knowledge transfer*—a field that simplifies the planned movement of critical knowledge and skills from subject matter experts to their coworkers. In other words, we replicate top technical talent. I've written two books on the subject and have run one of the world's leading knowledge transfer consulting companies since the early nineties. While we've solved knowledge transfer problems in the heart of blue-chip companies around the globe for many years, it turns out that having a great knowledge transfer process is only one piece of the talent risk management puzzle. The ability to assess and mitigate talent risk on an ongoing basis is the larger imperative. Through my firm's consulting work, I've found that giving organizations a better way to get at relevant talent data so they can talk about their risk and align on priorities is the greatest pain point we can remedy today.

In addition to my firm's real-world experiences and active research in the field, the assertions and models in this book are backed by a unique research study conducted in 2016 by the Institute for Corporate Productivity (i4cp), the nonprofit research arm of a large network of corporations across industries. The study revealed that about eight out of ten executives believe unaddressed talent risk poses "a serious threat" to their competitive advantage, innovation, and productivity. They said the greatest barrier to addressing their risk was they "don't have a feasible process for analyzing talent risk."[6] Executives simply don't know how to do this work. But the exciting news for me was that the study showed correlations between the talent risk framework I'm sharing here and high-performing organizations. You'll hear more about the research in later chapters and in Appendix II: About the Research.

---

6 "Preliminary Results: Talent Risk Management Survey," Institute for Corporate Productivity, March 2016.

HOW TO USE THIS BOOK

This book is for anyone who leads people at work. It will be especially valuable to business leaders who manage people with a high degree of technical or professional expertise. This includes scientists, engineers, operators, technicians, researchers, analysts, project managers, designers, inventors, and mechanics. Even though your technical experts and their work environments are often unique in the world, their risks are familiar, and the method to capture their relevant data and analyze the risk is remarkably the same.

In Part I, we'll discuss the talent risk problem and look at common myths around talent risk management. We will also discuss costs of not managing your talent risk and explore the relationships between the traditional fields of talent management, risk management, and strategic planning.

In Part II, we'll explore a better way to manage your talent risk. I'll explain a key obstacle—I call it the "technical fog"—that has stymied executive efforts to get a handle on their talent risk. I'll show you how to use a simple tool to lift this technical fog to get at the relevant data needed to fully and accurately analyze your talent risk. I'll walk you through how to get yourself and your peers aligned around which risks are high priorities. Then I'll lay out what I believe is the best solution for mitigating talent risk: structured knowledge transfer—a system based on the fundamentals of how people learn technical skills on the job. I'll also provide you with common business scenarios and the language for asking the *right* corresponding talent questions; then model the data-driven, clear answers you should be getting back.

In Part III, I'll share several case studies that present typical talent-related business problems and show you how some of the world's best companies solved these challenges using the talent risk framework. For additional case studies, you can go to www.steve trautman.com. Another appendix provides a simple exercise that you can do in sixty to ninety minutes that will transform how you view talent risk at your organization. The website also has additional tools, white papers, and resources on Talent Risk Management and Knowledge Transfer.

DON'T SETTLE

My challenge to you via this book? **Don't settle.**

- *Don't settle* for the lackluster results you have become accustomed to from your talent risk efforts.

- *Don't settle* for people telling you that you can't get at the detailed, relevant talent data you want to make informed business decisions.

- *Don't settle* for the groans of peers, teammates, and superiors who think that solid, clear, measurable talent risk management is not practical.

Instead, invest a little time and see a new way forward.

PART I

The Talent Risk Problem and Why Many Fail

CHAPTER 1

Eight Talent Risk Myths

THERE IS SOME IRONY WHEN EXECUTIVES SAY "PEOPLE ARE OUR MOST important asset," because everyone with a complicated workforce struggles to understand and manage this "most important" asset. Sure, organizations approach the problem with their best HR analytics or hope that a succession plan for the top executives and a little luck will carry them through. But even with all the effort expended, in the end, few can say with justifiable confidence that they will have the workforce they need to execute their business strategy three to thirty-six months from now.

I can't blame you for feeling confused and frustrated by this problem. How many times in the last thirty to forty years has a magical solution come down the pipeline only to be revealed as a giant "flavor of the month" flop? It often feels easier to assume there is no answer and just plow ahead with a big contingency budget and plenty of aspirin—even though you don't accept defeat so readily in other areas of business.

> It often feels easier to assume there is no answer and just plow ahead with a big contingency budget and plenty of aspirin—even though you don't accept defeat so readily in other areas of business."

I have found that many fail in this

space because of eight damaging talent risk myths. Let's dispel these misconceptions and clear a path for positive action.

TALENT RISK MYTH #1

"People issues" are inherently slippery and can't be managed with the same hard data that we require from every other part of our businesses.

Current attempts at managing talent risk, including competency models, demographic profiles, job ladders, and formal training, all fall short when it comes to measurably reducing your talent risks. What do you really know if you put a person on a job ladder, inventory their competencies, provide them with a proper performance review, and send them to training on some regular basis? Are you confident they will perform the work required of their role consistent with your expectations? I'm not arguing that there is no value in all this investment. The trouble is that it stops short of answering the fundamental question: Where is the data that proves you will have the technical workforce you need both now and in the future?

Imagine if the legal department decided that all the contracts were "probably fine" or the financials included "mostly accurate" numbers. Imagine if your suppliers said the order "might" be on the truck or your tax advisor said you "probably" won't go to jail for fraud. Who would settle for so much ambiguity? Yet when we talk about our people, we settle for gut feelings more often than not.

I recently had a lunch conversation with Kevin Oakes, the CEO of i4cp. His organization identifies best practices and next-gen ideas that fuel productivity and bottom-line results. He became quite animated when I raised the topic of managing talent risk. "Lately, talent risk is a notion that many of our member organizations have been strongly embracing," he said, "and that's being driven by their board of directors and senior leaders. At the board level, leaders are essentially saying, 'As we grow as an organization, how do we look at talent risk like we look at financial risk?'"

I will make the case that "people issues" are not an excuse for a lack of objective clarity. The truth is you can obtain hard technical capacity data on every employee at every level of the organization. You can expect to get a report that explains the talent risk profile of any team and how it has changed over the last three months. You can expect a new hire to be up to speed in half the time it currently takes—and measure the success or failure of onboarding. You can expect to know the potential cost of a mistake for people working in critical areas who are not fully prepared to work. You can expect every manager to be able to explain how they're maximizing their team's head count to bring full value to the bottom line. And you can expect all this data in an app like Excel with hard numbers—including dollar signs where appropriate. Don't settle for less.

TALENT RISK MYTH #2

**Technically capable people are too
complicated and emotional to be "produced"
the way a car can be manufactured. I've got to
let them do what they do their own best way.**

Over the last several decades, motivational speakers, consultants, thought leaders, and the like (read: people like me) have convinced us that, as executives, we must improve our "engagement scores" by helping our employees find their collective bliss. The idea is that if you give people enough freedom and opportunity, their unique path will unveil itself and they'll be fulfilled, happy, and productive.

Executives proudly trumpet that they "hire great people and then get out of their way." Bureaucracy is the devil, and if you cut all the red tape, you'll finally unleash the true potential of your team. You must give people the freedom to "fail early and fail often" if you want to spark innovation.

While there may have been plenty of great reasons to head toward these ideas in the past, the pendulum has swung too far in this direction. It has allowed business leaders to abdicate responsibility for setting clear expectations by saying stuff like "My people are unique and I would never want to treat them like robots."

For example, I was on the phone recently with a senior VP for a major hotel chain who listed a broad array of programs that were designed to usher about 1,000 back-office workers from the "old way" of working to the "new way." She had hired consultants to redesign the organization, had provided formal training to support a new workflow, and had trained all her managers to lead through the change. It all sounded good until she laid out the results of all this effort. They had been working at completing this transformation for *three years* and she still had substantial pockets of people who refused to make the shift. Too many claimed a lack of role clarity. Bastardized versions of the "new way" were springing up as people tried to cope with the extended period of transition. To add more fuel to the fire, she had just found out that she needed to plan for the acquisition of a major competitor. Still, she felt confident that if they "stayed the course" with the broad guidance they had set up, they would get through to the other side.

The truth is this executive didn't have a transition problem. She had a *production* problem. Much like a factory needs to produce high-quality cars, she needed to produce high-quality workers who could do the work the *right* way. What would happen if, when a car factory changed from one model year to the next, they let some of the workers continue to make last year's model? What if it was OK for some workers to bolt the steering wheel where the front tire belongs because that seemed best to them? What if we only told the workers what we *didn't like* about their output and never bothered to give them the hard data they needed to make the cars right in the first place? This is what was happening for this executive. She knew that plenty of people were doing things the *wrong* way, but when I asked her to put a stake in the ground and tell me who was *right*, she demurred. "We need to give people room," she said.

I realize that the idea of producing people like cars is radical—and may sound a little crazy. Well, what if being clear about constraints and being as exacting as new car specifications made our employees *more* engaged, happier, and likely to stay in their roles for longer periods of time? What if being clear about the *right way* to do the work freed them up to be more creative in areas where innovation is welcome, because they aren't spending endless hours in meetings where no one makes a decision, or cleaning up messes because the standards were never clear in the first place? In a factory, no one would settle for a production line that was still making poor-quality cars after three years. Why settle for less when looking at managing your technical talent? With the right framework and process, technical talent can be developed and replicated much like a production model.

TALENT RISK MYTH #3

Having a succession plan for top executives is enough talent risk management.

As I've worked with and studied organizations around the world, succession planning for top executives is clearly the most evolved form of talent risk management that I see. There are many forms of "high potential" lists and regular meetings of senior executives who talk over who could replace them if needed. Rotational programs are set up to provide broad experience with the business, including stints living abroad and lateral moves intended to fill gaps in a resume. Big organizations host events to encourage upcoming leaders to network, build relationships, and settle in for a long and successful career. Senior leaders I meet are often proud of their succession plans and feel confident they have the problem covered—but do they really?

I want to address this myth in two parts: the myth that current succession plans for senior leaders are enough and the myth that succession plans should stop at leadership instead of being developed for all critical employees, including many who aren't on the leadership track at all.

From what I've observed, succession plans for senior leaders work *around* the actual risk. These plans provide opportunities to *build* readiness but do little to *validate* readiness. For example, we're working with an SVP for a major digital imaging company who would like to retire or at least move to more of an "emeritus" status by the end of the year. His successor has been chosen and "groomed," but there are still reservations about the successor's ability to take over. The plan was to "give her another year to prove herself" but there was no clear measure of readiness. The SVP of HR said, "We'll just have to see."

In this book, I'll show you how we gave the successor a way to prove her readiness with a plan that is measurable and won't take a year to complete. It doesn't replace the existing succession planning programs but validates their efficacy in plain language. The truth is that there is no need to "wait and see" if the succession plan is working. We can prove it.

My second point regarding the value of current succession plans is that it is considered acceptable to stop succession planning at some level of senior leadership—usually at the VP or GM level. This means that there are no succession plans for the technical experts and other frontline employees who often pose a greater material risk to the business than their bosses on the twenty-ninth floor. I've seen a $50 million revenue stream put at risk because one software architect was hired away by a competitor before he could finish rolling out his product. Succession plans should be in place for all critical roles. In the 2016 i4cp research study on talent risk, one of the top five best practices identified for effectively addressing talent risk was "having succession plans for technical/professional experts."[7] It is a myth that this is too complicated an undertaking. The truth is you can create succession plans for every critical role, including your technical talent, so you can manage your talent risk regardless of job title or level.

TALENT RISK MYTH #4

You think you've been clear about what you need in terms of technical/professional talent because you've laid out a head count budget and org chart.

It certainly makes sense to start with a head count budget when thinking about talent. As you build out your business plan, you have to figure out how many people it is going to take to get the job done and at what cost. Your plan might include a need for one hundred engineers, ten project managers, fifteen business analysts, twenty quality experts, and so on. You'll probably need eight managers and a director to lead the charge. Then you can clarify even further and note that some of them should be "experienced" so they'll cost a little more. You can outsource some of it to a country with lower wages so there might be some savings there. The trouble is that, like boxes on an org chart, head count budget is only a shadow of the data you need to ensure that you have a sufficiently low talent risk profile.

One of the reasons for this is because not all "senior employees"

---

7   "Talent Risk," survey results presentation by the Institute for Corporate Productivity, April 2016.

are created equal. No surprise there. But if you are looking at head count as job titles on an org chart, hash marks on a job ladder, or lines in a budget, you're treating your experts as if that is all they are. Some have common skill sets that are appropriate for "plug and play" roles. However, those that impact your talent risk profile have unique knowledge and skills that make them—and only them—critical to your success. Yes, you can prepare a budget for these folks. But if you don't know what they really do for you, you don't understand the risks associated with each one if they transfer, take a redefined job role, or leave. You may find later that the risk was too high. For example, one of our client CIOs needed a top expert repurposed to a pet project of his. He could see from the org chart that the team was fully staffed, so he figured he could help himself to one of the senior guys. The team obviously had plenty to spare. The result? The expert's former team called him back to his old job so often that he had a foot in two worlds and was failing at both. The CIO thought there would be some howling about the move but he never expected to destabilize an entire technical team and put his own pet project at risk.

If he could have zoomed in on the unique roles the senior engineer played on the team, he could have realized the potential impact. The data he could have gathered would have suggested a five-week phased transition with a hard stop rather than an immediate pullout followed by endless "quick questions" from the old team. He would have been able to weigh the technical talent implications to both the existing team and the new project and timed the transition for a successful changeover. He could have used more complete data to manage his talent risk relative to his business need.

TALENT RISK MYTH #5

A reorganization to centralize or
decentralize your specialists—the age-old
"inhale vs. exhale" cycle of reorgs—is the
best way to reduce your technical talent risk.

Many organizations ping-pong between two imperfect organizational structures. In one model, they have all the people in one job family centralized into a single organization and then deploy experts to projects around the company as needed. In the other model, those same people report into their project/functional teams; the only thing they share with their job family counterparts is their title and sometimes a dotted line relationship with a "center of excellence" for their role.

Both scenarios present problems. If everyone is centralized, they lose touch with the business units they're supposed to understand and serve. If everyone is decentralized, they lose touch with their technical counterparts and deliver inconsistent results. In response to either of these problems, many organizations do what I call the "inhale or exhale reorg." The inhale reorg pulls all the members of a job family back into a central team so they can have more "synergies." The exhale reorg blows these same people back into functional teams so they can be "more connected to the core business." It is common to see the inhale or the exhale happen every two to three years.

I'm betting most of you have been a part of one of these inhale or exhale reorgs in the last five years. It is particularly common when a new executive takes over and is trying to shake things up. I saw that in action recently with an HR exec who wanted to make sure that all her employees were being better business partners, so she had them report to their line-of-business execs with a dotted line back to her. This was not a bad idea at all. In this case, the HR business partners really did need to get closer to their customers. The myth is that changing reporting relationships is *enough* to solve the problem of being sufficiently "connected" to either the job family or the functional org. Just because you are a member of an "HR Business Partner Job Family" (inhale), or you are the "HR Business Partner on the Acme 3000 team" (exhale), doesn't go nearly far enough to clarify the best way to be successful.

The truth is that—regardless of where someone sits and reports in the org structure—the best way to ensure their work is efficient, consistent with their peers, and highly connected to the business is to clarify expectations and give them an unambiguous plan for their success. In this book, I'll show you how to clarify in plain language exactly what is expected, not only for whole technical job families but for the individual and unique roles within each job family—even for your most specialized, highly technical experts. Whether you are a member of a centralized or decentralized team, you can and will be successful. And you won't have to put up with being inhaled or exhaled every two to three years to get there.

TALENT RISK MYTH #6

Our technical experts like being indispensable. We can't manage their technical risk because they think knowledge is power and won't share their knowledge.

This is probably the most common misconception I hear. The story usually includes a famous expert who is a genius but simply will not cross-train or transfer his knowledge to others. Years ago, I asked to be introduced to one such expert who embodied this issue perfectly. His manager pointed at a man behind a gunmetal gray desk in the corner and said to me, "That's Bob. He hates people, but he's our best guy. He won't help you unless you drag the information out of him. As far as I can tell, he hopes to die while working at his desk and wants to be left alone between now and then." OK, maybe I exaggerate exactly what the boss said, but it was close and you have to admit it isn't too hard to believe.

You probably have several "Bobs" in your technical team. Nearly everyone does. Well, I asked to be introduced to Bob and I offered to buy him a cup of coffee. When we sat down, I said, "Bob, folks around here think you hate people and you're not interested in teaching what you know. They say you believe that knowledge is power and you don't want to give up any of your power. What is your side of that story?"

Bob looked me in the eye, sighed, and said, "You know what, Steve—I've been here a long time. And after I had been here for about ten years, people started asking me to explain my work to them. Back then, I really tried. Sometimes I'd spend half of a day with someone trying to explain what I do. But, at the end of the day, two things would be true: They'd have learned almost none of what I was trying to teach, and they would basically hate my guts. After awhile, I decided to just skip the part where I spent half of a day and go directly to, 'They've learned nothing and hate my guts.' It was just faster. And besides, whose job is it to learn from me? None of these kids care about what I'm doing. And if they did, what out of everything I know should I teach them, and how would I fit that into my busy schedule? My managers will sometimes say, 'Can you let this kid follow you around while you teach him everything?' That is a tall order for a guy who's been around for decades and is already swamped."

I've told that story hundreds of times, because it is representative of most businesses and points out the obvious management issues. Bob is not the problem. *His boss is.* His boss isn't doing the work to mitigate the talent risk associated with Bob's unique knowledge. If you were Bob's boss, I would ask you:

- To whom should he transfer his knowledge? Has anyone told that person it is their *job* to learn from Bob?

- Precisely what do you want Bob to teach this coworker to *do*?

- How should he prioritize transferring knowledge relative to his regular workload? How much time should he spend doing one versus the other?

- If Bob doesn't instinctively know how to teach, what tools and techniques are you giving him to organize his knowledge into manageable chunks so he can deliver the information efficiently?

- Is he on his own to drive this? What role is his coworker playing in actively extracting the technical knowledge from him?

The truth is that the myth of the knowledge-hoarding expert is really covering up a management problem around how to direct and enable employees to share knowledge. All of these questions above are management's responsibility to answer and can be done so in plain language. We will discuss the concept of knowledge transfer as a way to mitigate risk in chapter 7. By the way, after we showed Bob's manager how to answer these questions and Bob how to teach his coworkers clearly, Bob ended up being an excellent and enthusiastic mentor to the "kid" assigned to him.

TALENT RISK MYTH #7

**It is impossible to "lift the technical fog"
for people like scientists, engineers, inventors,
technicians, and operators. Their jobs are just
too complicated and unique.**

I promise to explain what I mean by the "technical fog" in chapter 4, but for now, suffice it to say that many executives know their most valuable technical people by a short label, like Raj is my "security guy" or Monique is my "database whiz." If you asked the executive to explain much of what Raj or Monique actually *does*, the fog would come rolling in pretty fast. They'd just say things like, "Monique just works her magic . . ."

Managing day to day without a granular view of the technical expertise of each critical employee is not a problem most of the time— but when it is a problem, it can be a big one and can happen very fast. Everyone knows that we don't buy insurance just so we can drive our cars every day. We buy insurance so that when we get in a wreck, we are covered.

The truth is that even the most technical of technical experts—the research and development professionals who are inventing new products, mechanics who can tell if a machine is operating well by the way it sounds, video game producers who make the game "fun," or engineers who know how to troubleshoot problems they've never seen before—are all knowable. They have to be, because their risks have the costliest potential impact on your business. The technical fog *can* be lifted by quickly analyzing the actual *work* each individual contributes to the business. This is also why ownership of talent risk management should never be shouldered primarily by Human Resources; it's beyond the scope of HR to know an employee's daily tasks and skills.

We can all agree that your people are unique and uniquely valuable. Just don't settle for the idea that they are so unique that they can't be known at all.

TALENT RISK MYTH #8

> **Addressing talent risk isn't my responsibility as a line-of-business leader. It is owned by HR, our VP of Learning/Corporate University, our risk assessment committee, or [insert your favorite scapegoat here].**

One of the challenges we faced in choosing a title for this book was whether to use the words "Talent" and "Management" in the same sentence. The fear was that there are still too many executives whose eyes glaze over when any whiff of HR presents itself. It isn't hard to see why. The administration and maintenance of the people part of any business includes a bureaucratic, time-consuming, and emotional load for any leader. Where's the fun in that? If an organization gets it right, no one really notices. You could call it table stakes. But if there are problems, heads can roll.

Evidence of this problem isn't simply anecdotal. The 2016 i4cp research study on talent risk examined the barriers to an organization addressing risk. About 40 percent of executives reported, "It is not clear who owns this problem internally."

So, who should own the problem of gathering, assessing, prioritizing, and actively mitigating talent risk?

The truth is that you cannot expect the leaders around you—whether they are at the top of the food chain or on the front line—to be predictably good. They're usually well intentioned and hard working, but that doesn't mean they're effective. I say this because if you're looking for someone to solve your talent risk problem, it might as well be you. It doesn't matter where you sit on the org chart—high or low, HR or Line of Business—it is your responsibility as a leader to understand the risks your team or organization faces.

Why? Because addressing talent risk is particularly important for every operationally oriented business leader who is responsible for their team meeting business goals day to day and year to year. You can't hit your targets without the right team doing the right work. This is especially critical for people like CIOs, CTOs, COOs, CFOs, and senior VPs whose teams handle a great deal of specialized, technical, business-critical knowledge.

> " You can't hit your targets without the right team doing the right work. This is especially critical for people like CIOs, CTOs, COOs, CFOs, and senior VPs whose teams handle a great deal of specialized, technical, business-critical knowledge."

CHAPTER 2

The Cost of a Mistake

A $100,000 MISTAKE MIGHT BE A ROUNDING ERROR FOR A BIG FIRM, but a $1 million mistake usually gets everyone's attention. Costly mistakes happen when people go to work before they are sufficiently prepared to do their work well—before they *know* how to do the work properly. I'm not talking about just being inefficient. I'm talking about taking an action that has direct, unnecessary costs in the form of money, time, quality, and/or safety. In this chapter, I want you to see how these mistakes are readily predicted and, once you learn how to predict them, how you can prioritize and solve costly talent-related mistakes before they happen. By gathering a little bit of data and then using the data in everyday conversations led by any employee at any level of the organization, managing talent risk becomes a mindset and a practice that can slipstream into any culture.

To calculate the cost of a mistake, you break a role down into small enough increments that you can zoom in on the potentially expensive problems and ensure your people are prepared to avoid them. This doesn't have to be onerous. It is a way of thinking that anyone can be taught to follow.

I've done this exercise for some of the most unusual and complex jobs in the world, but to illustrate my point, I'm going to use remodeling a kitchen as a more familiar example. If you're the contractor running the project, you can start by making a list of all the big areas of expertise that come together to make a project like that work. It probably includes electrical, plumbing, ventilation, cabinetry, flooring, etc. Once you spend a few minutes getting those areas of expertise worked out, then you can look at each area and make a list of the skills needed to perform each job. What does the electrician do? What does the plumber do? What does the flooring guy do? You're starting to zoom in on the risks.

Let's take flooring and zoom in further. Here's a list of fifteen things the flooring expert might do:

1. Select appropriate flooring for the space.

2. Select appropriate fasteners and adhesives for the material.

3. Hire a subcontractor to install the flooring.

4. Protect the walls while the flooring is being installed.

5. Provide specialty tools for the flooring installation.

6. Order the flooring.

7. Deliver the flooring.

8. Demolish and remove the old flooring.

9. Prepare the subfloor before installing the new flooring.

10. Design the flooring pattern.

11. Install the flooring.

12. Choose a finish for the flooring.

13. Coat the flooring with the finish.

14. Troubleshoot problems with the flooring and finish.

15. Maintain job site.

Now that you have a better understanding of what the expert actually does, you only have to ask one question to figure out the cost of a mistake: If someone does anything on this list badly, what would it cost?

In every instance, a mistake is going to have a measurable cost:

- Money—restocking fees, overtime, paying twice for the same task, penalties, legal fees

- Time—slipped schedule, working late, not able to go to the next job

- Quality—rework, unhappy client, loss of referral, reputation

- Safety—loss of a worker, distraction, penalties, legal fees, reputation, death

To have a successful flooring project, myriad tasks must be done to a high standard—or the entire project is at risk. Calculating the cost of a mistake for each of these tasks allows the project manager to reduce risk in a methodical way so the odds of having a happy customer, hitting the schedule, and making a profit on the job are increased.

Experienced project managers think about this all day long. It is like breathing. They know that not delivering the materials on time could delay a whole job site for a day. How many men or women would not be productive because their materials got there late? What will it cost if someone damages the walls during floor demolition and you have to repair them? What happens to the schedule if the demo crew leaves a mess and the installers can't start until the mess is cleaned up? What if someone gets hurt in the demolition process? What if someone misses a quality control check that isn't found until after the owner has moved in? Now you are fixing a problem amid furniture, boxes, dogs, and children when you could have done an inexpensive fix before moving day.

In a matter of minutes, you can go from the project view—where you see the areas of expertise—to zoom in on individual tasks where you can then add up the cost of doing the task badly. At each level, you can gather data and use it to improve performance.

CALCULATE THE COST OF EVERYDAY MISTAKES

Let's look at a common task like leading a team meeting. What's the cost of running a team meeting badly? Let's add it up. Ten people attend the team meeting. They make on average $100,000 a year. Their hourly rate is about $50 an hour. That means that meeting costs $500 an hour.

When you count up $500 an hour, you think that $500 is not that big of a deal—except they have that team meeting every week. Now we've got $2,000 a month, which becomes $24,000 a year just for that one meeting. Oh, but it turns out those same ten people are not only in a single team meeting; they're in *eight* meetings each week.

When you gather the data, you start to realize the cost of leading a meeting badly could be as much as $500 an hour times eight hours a week times fifty weeks out of the year. If even half of these meetings are badly run, you're still looking at a $100,000 cost to the organization. Now we have a value proposition for improving the quality of the team meeting because it's so expensive to have all those people sitting around in a poorly run meeting.

The Cost of a Mistake Is Not Just Measured in Dollars

The complete cost of our people's mistakes is not just measured in dollars. Our avoidable mistakes are expensive in time, productivity, lost customers, lack of competitiveness, damaged reputations, and brand loyalty. What we're really talking about here is what some call *the cost of non-quality.*[8]

---

8   For a "Cost of a Mistake" calculator, go to www.stevetrautman.com.

Productivity Loss and Shutdowns

We met with a global company that makes compressed gas for a wide range of tanks—some might be small enough to fit on your back, like medical oxygen, or they might be a giant propane tank at an industrial site. Over the last couple of decades, they've automated their plants to a very high degree. Some plants don't even have people working there. Instead, they have somebody who is itinerant and moves between plants.

Automation like this is fantastic for reducing costs in many ways. But there are always a few people who can't be replaced with automation (yet)—like the mechanic or technician who, if a pump goes out or a valve is broken, is the one to call. They have two of these service technicians who had worked together for forty years. They retired on the same day, closing the door and turning off the lights on long, successful careers. Nobody really knew what these guys did, but the company figured the timing would probably be OK.

It didn't take long for their management to realize just how big the impact would be. It was as if no one else knew how to "turn the lights on." If you can't turn the lights on, you can't produce compressed gas. I asked the senior vice president, "What was the cost of that mistake?" He said, "Well, the plant was down for three months, so more than a million dollars. And the trouble is, I have twelve more plants with a version of the same two guys keeping things running."

Mismanaging a talent risk like this can mean not only plant shutdowns but also a cascading productivity loss if that plant serves other parts of your business or major customers.

It's Not Just People Leaving

The cost of a single person leaving is usually an easy calculation. But what about the times when you *really* don't know your talent? Acquisitions pose a different talent risk, and this is where the board steps in. The co-chair of the National Association of Corporate Directors

(NACD) blue-ribbon committee report on the board's role in talent development[9] says that boards can play a critical role in managing talent risk after an acquisition. "In a merger or acquisition it is important to talk about talent because these deals are often a major capital allocation, and the risk of the deal failing due to talent risk can be high. Boards may wish to visit newly acquired sites and meet key talent—not just top officers, but also top young talent who are critical to the future of the organization."

Safety Incidents and Costs in Human Life

Safety is the one talent risk area that is routinely managed with data already. Any industrial site will have a safety culture backed up by facts; they prioritize and mitigate risk every day because the cost of a mistake is potentially injury or death. But safety isn't measured only in injuries. It also impacts productivity and retention—which have a direct impact on business success. For example, at one of our clients' facilities, a copper mine in Arizona, we were brought in by the safety professionals. Their data said that new employees were more likely to get hurt during their first ninety days on the job than were their more experienced counterparts. And once an employee experienced a safety incident, he or she was far more likely to quit than their new-hire peers. The cost of a mistake in this instance was the loss of a valuable worker during a time when it was extremely difficult to find talent in the first place.

Inconsistencies, Rework, and Poor Quality

One common scenario among our clients is outsourcing and/or offshoring work. Since the work needs to be done properly by the outsourcing partner, their employees must be trained to do it to standards. The question is: How are you going to get them up to speed? If

---

9   "BRC Talent Development: A Boardroom Imperative," The National Association of Corporate Directors, 2013.

job shadowing is the method for onboarding, then you have to send them somebody they can shadow.

If your expert wants to go, you are probably fine except that she isn't working on her domestic projects while she's overseas. The expert knows all the stuff the new people will need to learn, and you know the training will be top-notch. The trouble starts when the expert is unwilling or unable to go. What happens when you can't do without that person stateside for that length of time? Or if he doesn't want to be away from his family for that long? Then whom do you send? Often the person who gets sent is the person who's *willing to go*. And that person is rarely the expert. You're replicating the person who happens to be available versus the person who is actually best at the role. What is the cost of a mistake when you replicate the wrong person? Can you afford inconsistencies and lesser-quality work? Are you setting yourself up for rework or other hidden costs?

Measuring the Wrong Thing

One of our online video game clients has a large tote board in its bull pen—the room where many of the software developers and gamers work. There are about sixty people in the room. Even with all the noise and commotion, the tote board is hard to miss.

Anytime a player (their customers) does something on the game that requires them to spend money to get ahead—the fee is perhaps a nickel—the tote board total goes up. Everybody's face is literally staring at the revenue stream, and their job is clearly to make the numbers on that board move. I was talking to a key expert in the bull pen about talent risk. I said to her, "If we do knowledge transfer, we're going to replicate you, and then we're going to get twenty people in this room to be more like you. That's going to make you more efficient, more effective. It's also going to take the pressure off you."

She looked deeply into my eyes and said, "Steve, if I have a choice between making a nickel on that board today or making $1,000 tomorrow, I will make the nickel on the board today *because that's what I'm measured on."* That was the culture of the entire place. Everything was short-term revenue, short-term revenue, short-term revenue. Making the case that if you invest an hour, you save ten just did not fly with anybody in the organization. I could tell because that tote board was up there just counting the nickels.

The person who's making the business case has to say the best use of my/our/your time is to invest in solving this problem so that the cost of a mistake will be reduced over the long haul. People make that tradeoff every day. We all have too much work to do. We have to pick the thing we do that's the highest value. In this instance, instead of looking at the nickel as a problem, we're going to look at the cost of thirty people doing the wrong thing for a month.

Damaged Brand Image and Customer Dissatisfaction

The industry is oil and gas. The projects being sold by vendors in this industry are major industrial installations like a refinery or a floating oil rig. These are megaprojects that come together over the course of several years. The clients are Big Oil—Shell, Chevron, British Petroleum, and the like.

For the client, there are obvious risks to their brand. Think about the Deepwater Horizon Macondo exploration well that blew up in the Gulf of Mexico in 2010. Cleanup, along with environmental and economic damages and penalties levied on BP, was over USD 50 billion. Plus, the company's name will be forever linked with the disaster.

Not all oil and gas projects have such a spectacular history. However, they all face schedule risks and cost overruns. The scope and size of the projects are incredibly expensive, and there are huge implications to making a mistake there. Clients work hard to reduce their risk profiles through guarantees from their vendor.

Clients are starting to say, "Before I sign the contract with you, I want to interview the person who is going to be the senior project engineer of this whole project. I want a DNA sample and a thumb-print because I want the person you promised for the duration. Don't introduce me to one leader, and then bait-and-switch with some other executive once the project is up and running. The risks are too high." If you do not have experts prepared for and committed to the job, the client will go elsewhere.

WE HAVE MONEY TO FIX THE PROBLEM, SO IT ISN'T A PROBLEM

One final story gets to the insidious reason the cost-of-a-mistake problems go unsolved. This story speaks to a culture of solving problems rather than preventing them. I was recently in a meeting with fifteen VPs from around the world who are responsible for procurement and cost management for multibillion-dollar construction contracts. We put them through a twenty-minute "cost of a mistake" exercise and uncovered over $13 million worth of *routine* mistakes made at different stages of their projects by procurement staff who were not fully prepared to take on their roles. As they were creating the list (a few line items are shown in the following table), I jumped in several times to say I thought they were exaggerating the cost of each mistake. Each time they pushed back and said, "It's *at least* that much!" I remember standing there with my jaw on the ground. These executives had just made a list of over $13 million worth of mistakes *routinely* made by their own employees on a typical project, and they didn't seem the least bit shocked.

I said, "OK, good, I know exactly how to solve this problem. This is a knowledge transfer problem. We'll figure out who in your workforce is the expert for each task contributing to the $13 million. Then, we'll get the rest of your people quickly trained up to be consistent with the expert so they don't make these avoidable mistakes. We can get a plan in place that makes sure new hires learn the right way to work so you can avoid the problem in the future. I

Phase of Project	Business Problem	How It Manifests	Cost	Notes
Proposal	Lack of Skill	Key info missed in proposal review phase	$250,000.00	
Initiate (Handover)	Lack of Skill	Inaccurate estimate	$100,000.00	Rework (or extra work) and more people on the project that weren't planned
Execution	Lack of Skill	Late warning because we did not detect a trend	$225,000.00	3 months of rework
Execution	Lack of Skill	Inaccurate budget (underestimated)	$1,000,000.00	Cost overrun; but a skilled cost controller can make a recommendation to the PM to change strategy
Execution	Lack of Skill	Change order Management	$1,000,000.00	Could "leave money on the table." Might under-recover the cost of that change
Execution	Lack of Skill	Construction evaluate a subcontractor	$1,000,000.00	Would have to pay too much money to the subcontractor
Execution	Lack of Skill	Mis-forecasts engineering	$10,000.00	Can't provide an early warning that allows engineering to be more efficient
Execution	Lack of Skill	Handover of estimate from proposal to execution	$10,000,000.00	Spending contingency
Execution	Lack of Skill	Poor quality PMR	$100,000.00	Takes more work hours (should be done in one day)
Close out	Lack of Skill	Not giving feedback into estimating	???	Inaccurate cost estimation mistakes repeated in future proposals
Running Total				
			$13,685,000.00	

Figure 1. Talent challenges and their cost impact

just need a sponsor. You'll all benefit from this project because you all have teams making the same mistakes around the world. I just need one of you to greenlight a $200,000 project so we can solve this $13,000,000+ problem that's happening over and over again." Not a single executive raised their hand.

It turned out they had a contingency budget for fixing the mistakes after they happened but no money to preemptively fix the mistakes in the first place. They seemed more content to hemorrhage the money than to start down the road to risk mitigation. If I hadn't been there myself, I wouldn't have believed it.

The resistance was not stemming from a lack of faith in the proposed solution. We had more than enough evidence that our talent risk mitigation efforts would work. We'd already completed a successful project within that company with job roles that were frankly much more complex than those here. The roadblock was that no budgets were set up for managing talent risk. There were only budgets set up for contingency.

Unfortunately, this story is hardly unique. People are more accustomed to (and, as a result, more comfortable with) firefighting than fire prevention. People have gotten comfortable spending contingency budgets, but they're not always comfortable with spending money on being as preemptive as possible—which is effectively what risk management is. You're trying to prevent the fire instead of reactively fighting the fire. Somehow, prevention goes against the corporate grain—perhaps due to a lack of clear talent risk management solutions that has lasted for decades.

WHO SHOULD BE HAVING THIS NEW CONVERSATION? EVERYONE.

Leading the cost-of-a-mistake conversation should be a universal skill. It's an incredibly useful tool for understanding the value of certain work. It's also handy for showing a cost-to-benefit ratio when you want to champion change that has a price tag attached. And, as we'll see in

Part II of this book, it's vital data for quantifying your talent risk and its financial impact. However, calculating the cost of a mistake is a political hot potato that few want to embrace. Talking about mistakes—even just possible ones—can be risky business in some organizations.

Instead, everybody should be eager and able to speak to the cost of a mistake. It should be one of the things that—and this is the radical shift that I'm proposing here—we *all* talk about. It becomes part of normal conversation. At the end of the day, management needs to create a culture that says "We're going to do a cost-of-a-mistake exercise. We're going to learn from it. All actions up to this day are given amnesty. They don't reflect poorly on you. Some costs may be embarrassing, but don't worry. We know how to fix them now. Going forward, this is how we are going to think. We're not only noticing that there's the potential for this cost of a mistake; we're actually going to fix these risks."

DON'T SETTLE
FOR AVOIDING THE HARD CONVERSATIONS

Expect to face some resistance when seeking data on and discussing the cost of mistakes in a preventative way in your organization. Be prepared to recognize the different ways people hide reasons for getting at and facing facts:

- People are embarrassed by the facts, the data.

- People are worried about being held accountable for something they don't feel they have control over.

- Cultural and systemic hurdles inhibit preventative action.

- People don't want to accept risk as part of their current reality. Instead, they only accept the current crisis as reality. The familiar crisis of today is easier to face than the approaching calamity of tomorrow.

WHEN YOU KNOW YOUR TALENT, YOU KNOW THE COST OF A MISTAKE

You can't know the true cost of a mistake until you understand what it is your experts actually do. I like to use the example of Simon, a sugar expert at a global confectionary company. He's known for picking the sugar for the next chocolate or biscuit product as it is in development. He does stuff like *"analyze the capacity of a vendor to provide enough sugar to supply this product line."*

What's the cost of a mistake if he misjudges a vendor? What if the supplier can't produce enough? You can imagine a salesman pushing his wares: "Hey, Simon, buy our sugar. We're awesome. We'll have you covered no matter what volume you demand." Simon hires them, and then they don't deliver.

The sugar—glucose syrup, actually—is for cookies and chocolate. The company Simon hired is supposed to deliver trainloads of that syrup, but, hey, they couldn't do it. Sorry. What happens? You have to find a backup supplier and find them now or risk shutting down production. The price will probably go up since it is a rush job now. You have to worry about quality. You have to worry about consistency because this guy was going to be supplying a consistent syrup. If the syrup changes, then do they have to rejigger the formulas in the rest of the product to get the chocolate bars to come out right? Will the taste change and upset customers? That one small thing balloons into a host of expensive problems pretty quickly. One little mistake in the list of all the things Simon does every day could shut down whole factories.

Simon also protects the company's intellectual property from the competition. Apparently, competitors would routinely send out moles in the guise of doing business with him when they were really gathering competitive intelligence. I mean, who knew? This seventy-year-old British guy who smells like Willy Wonka and eats too much junk food is actually sniffing out espionage. (You'll get to learn more about Simon's fascinating work in chapter 7.)

Instead of asking, "Who knew?" the better question is "Why didn't we know?"

One clear reason leaders fail at managing talent risk is that they stop short of assessing, discussing, and being transparent about the cost of unmitigated talent risk. This is a discipline that every leader can bring to the conversation.

In chapter 3, we'll look at how managing talent risk is best done at the intersection of traditional risk management, talent management, and strategic planning.

Technical Talent Risk Management—the Intersection of Strategy, Risk, and People

IF YOU MADE A LIST OF ALL THE OVERUSED YET POORLY UNDERSTOOD words in our business vocabulary, *strategy*, *risk*, and *people/talent* would be at the top. It isn't for lack of trying. Billions are spent every year in an effort to write and set strategy, assess and communicate risk, and take care of the human resources every organization relies on. Yet still we fall short. Strategies are unclear to the people who have to execute them, risks become realities in surprising ways, and the capacity of people to contribute goes unrealized.

Maybe one of the problems is that executives think about and work with these three concepts separately rather than in concert. In this chapter, I'd like to explore what would happen if we did a better job of managing the intersection between the three (see Figure 2).

OWNERSHIP OF THE INTERSECTION

Every major organization has owners for the spheres of Talent Management, Risk Management, and Strategic Planning—owners who survey the landscape, assess problems, provide insight, propose and implement solutions, and get paid to do it. But no one really owns the intersection of the three. Instead of yielding insight that provides a confident, guiding light for leaders at all levels, this intersection is gray and lifeless—or, even worse, a black hole that drains energy.

Figure 2. Talent risk management sits at the intersection of strategy, people, and risk. See Color Insert 1 for color version.

Recently I met with the new HR business partner for the CIO of a Fortune 500 manufacturer. She described the "skill committee" meeting she had just attended as a "room full of some of our best technical leaders completely wasting their time trying to solve a problem everyone can see but no one can explain. It was awful . . . " Does this sound familiar?

Her comment illustrated why this intersection isn't at the heart of leadership conversations every day. It shows why there aren't fireworks, insight, and practical solutions where these three critical disciplines meet: No one knows how to make it happen.

To make things even more complex, add a *technical talent* overlay to this concept and you can see how grave the implications are. Every major organization has their own form of technicians in IT, Engineering, Research, Finance, Sales, and Operations. Even in the best of circumstances, adding technical talent to the mix of Talent Management, Strategic Planning, and Risk Management creates a jumble of confusing, frustrating, and ever-changing targets. How can boards, executives, and other leaders understand and *measure* whether or not they are managing the intersection of talent, risk, and strategy in a meaningful way?

We have to find this intersection quickly by taking the best of all three disciplines and setting a high standard for utility. Talent risk data must be measurable and clear, predictive, quick to gather, and easy to maintain while still being comprehensive enough to guide well-informed decisions.

Let's look at how the three separate disciplines—Strategic Planning, Risk Management, and Talent Management—are already working together and where they have room to bring more value.

THE INTERSECTION OF STRATEGIC PLANNING AND RISK MANAGEMENT

Leaders in Enterprise Risk Management (ERM) would argue that they have this intersection worked out already, and they are right—to a point. The Committee of Sponsoring Organizations of the Treadway Commission (COSO) provides a great overview of ERM:

> *Enterprise risk management is more than a risk listing. Managing risk across an organization requires more than listing the "top 10" risks or making an inventory of all risks within the organization. Enterprise risk management is broader and includes practices that management puts in place to actively manage risk to appropriate levels. Enterprise risk management addresses more than internal*

control. Internal control is an integral subset of enterprise risk management. But enterprise risk management also addresses other topics such as setting strategy, governance, communicating with stakeholders, and measuring performance. Its principles apply at all levels of the organization and across all functions.[10]

This approach to risk management helps business leaders analyze, prioritize, mitigate, inform, and monitor the risk that their strategy will fall flat. ERM typically includes business resiliency checklists that have something like the following line item to address technical talent:

Identify Required Skill Sets and Staff Allocation—this is the time to identify the number of staff and which skills you require to perform and maintain those essential services/ functions.[11]

Of course, this step in the checklist makes great sense and everyone would agree that it should be done, but the plans fall apart when you go on to ask, "How, exactly, do we identify the required skill sets and staff allocation?" Again, if you add the word "technical" into the equation, this becomes even more daunting. Is it good enough to have a great intersection between strategy and enterprise risk that doesn't have a sufficient view of the risk your technical talent brings to the equation?

THE INTERSECTION OF RISK MANAGEMENT AND TALENT MANAGEMENT

Business leaders manage strategic, financial, and operational risks every day with the kind of rigor that befits their potential for things to go wrong.

---

10 "Public Exposure: Enterprise Risk Management—Aligning Risk with Strategy and Performance," June 2016 Edition, Committee of Sponsoring Organizations of the Treadway Commission.
11 "A Checklist for a Resilient Business Continuity Plan," Dynamic Strategies, June 2016.

As you know from your own experience—and as I'll show you throughout this book—technical talent risk is not managed as methodically. To illustrate my point, let's look at what would happen if manufacturing executives (for example) managed their operational risk in the way that they manage talent risk today.

- First, they'd count the number of buildings and machines that make up their factories and be pleased with themselves that they know how many they have.

- Then, they'd ask the leaders to list the machines they think are really good at their jobs so they could be rotated to new locations in the plant.

- Some of the special machines would get extra oil during their annual maintenance.

- When one machine went out of service, all of the managers would stand around and try to figure out what that machine used to do and if it really mattered in the first place.

- When a new machine was purchased, they'd set it next to an old machine and hope it figured out what to do.

- When a machine performed improperly, they'd spend whatever money it took to fix the errant output and allay customer dissatisfaction, but they'd never recalibrate the machine because they wouldn't want to appear to micromanage.

- When they needed a machine in a different plant, they'd pull an "experienced" machine out of a current assembly line and hope the other machines in that line would "pick up the slack."

Of course, human beings are not machines, and it would be a mistake to treat them like they are. But they're not so mysterious that we can't take a lesson from operations risk management. Is it good enough to manage people risk—especially those with valuable technical talent and knowledge—with anything other than the hard data that typically accompanies other kinds of risk management?

> " Is it good enough to manage people risk—especially those with valuable technical talent and knowledge—with anything other than the hard data that typically accompanies other kinds of risk management?"

THE INTERSECTION OF STRATEGIC PLANNING AND TALENT MANAGEMENT

Executives are frequently frustrated that their organizations do not really "get" the strategy. The problem manifests itself in a variety of ways. You think your people appear inwardly focused, take too long to get new ideas to market, can't hit their margin targets, or frustrate rather than delight their customers. And, just maybe, they think you didn't do a very good job of explaining the strategy and how they fit into the big picture. No matter how brilliant an executive's vision is for the organization, there is no value if that vision cannot be translated into a strategy and operational plans that are readily executed by the front line.

There are many ways that executives communicate their strategy—including producing everything from a one-page bulleted list, to a dense document worthy of a doctoral thesis, to a cartoonlike drawing meant to tell the story so clearly that even a child could understand. And there are many ways to "roll out" the strategy and motivate people to lean in and get it done. These include town hall presentations, social media campaigns, formal training, inspiring posters, presentations from customers, and T-shirts for all.

I won't argue which of these approaches is most worthy, but I will suggest that they typically fall short in the intersection of strategy and people. To fully understand if your strategy is at risk of failure, you have to measure whether it has been internalized and can be executed by every employee. Here is the litmus test: Once the strategy has been in circulation for thirty days, can every frontline employee answer three questions?

1. How do I fit in the big picture relative to this new strategy?

2. What are my tasks?

3. How do I know if I'm doing them right?

If the strategy is clear, then getting every employee to have a personal answer to these three questions is not a pipe dream. It is absolutely possible. We'll talk more about how to get everyone on the same page concerning your strategy in chapter 8. For now, it's important to ask: Is it good enough to have a great strategy if you can't measure the risk that it's well understood and can be executed properly and predictably?

THE INTERSECTION OF STRATEGY, RISK, AND TALENT

Executives do not have to settle for clarity in two out of these three elements. You're not getting the insight you should expect because you're not asking for it and/or your people do not know how to give it to you. Executives who want to ensure whether they are truly managing their technical talent risk should be able to ask these questions and get clear, measurable answers:

From your strategic planners—

- What is the strategy?

- How are you communicating it to the front line?

- How are you measuring that it has been received and can be executed by every employee in the organization?

From your talent managers—

- What specific technical expertise is required to execute our strategy?

- How many people will I need with those technical skills?

- What is the risk that I won't have enough of those people ready to execute our strategy?

From your risk managers—

- How are you measuring, tracking, and reporting on my technical talent risk?

- What are the potential costs of these risks?

- What investments are being made to drive talent risk reduction?

For all three disciplines, answering these questions provides a terrific way to add value and serve as true business partners. Talent management leaders should be excited because it gives added relevance to their efforts. Risk management leaders should love it because it makes their work more about the future and not just about finding problems. And strategic planners should love it because it's going to make their strategy more likely to be executed successfully.

The first step in this journey is recognizing that Talent Risk Management is a young, burgeoning field that may sound familiar because it draws on all three disciplines, but—in reality—it is its own unique discipline. And since it sits at the *intersection* of these three disciplines, it is currently a no-man's-land in terms of clear ownership. Starting at the board and working all the way down to every level of leadership, this discipline needs to be woven into the rhythm of every business interaction. No strategy or plan should be approved, no budget set, no priority negotiated without first taking a clear-eyed look at data to illuminate the talent implications. This is a field whose time has come.

Ownership of talent risk should not rest in any one of the three disciplines. Instead, it should rest with the most senior executives. With this perspective, each executive can confidently say—

- Here is my strategy . . .

- Here are my people . . .

- Here is how we know we're going to make it happen . . .

In the following pages, we're going to take the black hole and turn it into a framework and a plan that leaders from the board to the front line can get behind and do something about.

The Talent Risk Solution

CHAPTER 4

The Importance of Lifting
the Technical Fog

A NEWLY APPOINTED EXECUTIVE AT A MAJOR STEEL MANUFACTURER
needed to reduce employee costs. Looking at org charts from the company's fifteen locations, he quickly spotted the same team of technical specialists at every location—regardless of the work going on at
each location. If he reorganized those fifteen teams into one central
technical team, the savings would be substantial on multiple levels. With org charts in hand, it was easy to see where he could move
employees, and he was counting on the managers to help him identify the low-performing technicians. He knew there would be some
challenges, but his mandate of reducing head count was clear. Not
unexpectedly, the leaders and technical experts on his team tried to
talk him out of the changes. He heard their concerns but felt that he
needed to take a stand.

The executive understood the organizational charts but had no
real understanding of the technical expertise behind the job titles.
We ran some talent risk scenarios for him, and the data proved that
the reorg as originally envisioned would be a *disaster*. The moves that
had seemed so obvious would have cut the very people who ran core

systems. He was not the first leader to nearly fall into this trap. Historically, the most daunting step in managing talent risk is getting a clear and detailed view of the most complex and mission-critical work done in an organization. This is the poorly understood—and often undocumented—work that keeps the plant floors humming, the software running, research coming, distribution flowing, finance analyzing, and technicians operating. In a very real sense, if this work isn't done, your business grinds to a halt.

WHAT DO YOU REALLY KNOW ABOUT YOUR TECHNICAL EXPERTS?

Let's imagine you have two employees who are thinking about leaving your organization. The first is Enzo. He is being heavily recruited. The second is Adelaide. She is nearing retirement. Both have technical jobs, but it is hard to understand exactly what they do. However, they are both valued employees, so you have gathered quite a bit of information on each one.

Here is what you know about Enzo:

- He's a senior developer.

- He's been with you for twelve years.

- He's thirty-six years old.

- He's married with two kids receiving health benefits.

- He makes $142,000, which is within an appropriate salary range for his role.

- He has worked in your US HQ and your Singapore office.

- On Myers-Briggs he's an INTJ.

- He is the go-to guy for the ADM database and for the security protocols.

- His team thinks that if you lose him the place will shut down.

You have much of the same information for Adelaide. She is the research scientist responsible for working with the tissue samples in your biotech lab. She has been with you for years, so you are a bit more familiar with her work and also know the following about her:

- The tissue sample work is likely going to be the reason your products beat the competition.

- Once the tissue sample work is complete, it will be used by hundreds of people around the world, and the samples must all be tightly consistent with each other for the value to be fully realized.

- If anyone gets stuck with any problem, they go to Adelaide and she tells them what to do.

- She doesn't really document her work. It is mostly in her head.

- Adelaide has been with you long enough to retire with a full pension.

That's about all you can say. You know names, their place on the org chart, maybe some demographic info, and perhaps some vague competencies that they tested for along the way. In terms of their actual expertise, you have only a general headline: "He's our go-to guy for the ADM database and for the security protocols," or "She is the queen of tissue samples." The rest of their technical talent profile that tells us why they are so valuable is on the other side of what we in my consulting firm call *the technical fog*.

WHAT IS THE TECHNICAL FOG?

As the name implies, the technical fog is a murky barrier. Leaders sit on one side of the technical fog with the basic information I laid out above. On the other side, your most valued employees and contractors churn away on important tasks that hardly anyone but the workers themselves understand. Their relevant wisdom, tacit knowledge, and valuable secret sauce lie on their side of the fog.

The higher up you are as an executive, the murkier the fog. Maybe you can kind of squint and see through it a little. Maybe you have some context so the outlines and the shadows are possible to discern, but there's no way for you to really know more than that. Yet your business is dependent on the Enzos and Adelaides of the world. You're at the mercy of their ability and willingness to come to work every day and deliver.

That is the risk. This technical fog makes it seem impossible to inventory, analyze, discuss, and replicate the complex and specialized work done by these skilled workers. It's the reason why so many line executives and HR departments struggle mightily to get a handle on their talent risks. The risk is not visible in the demographic profiles or competency models. It resides in the detailed data about an individual worker's expertise, knowledge, and skills. It's why the plant is shut down, the customer is disappointed, and the costly mistake is made. It's where the competition sneaks in and takes your business.

So, what should you do about that?

LIFTING THE TECHNICAL FOG

As I explained earlier, one of our clients had two senior mechanics retire in the same month. Usually that wouldn't be an issue, but they both worked in a gas compression plant where automation and outsourcing had reduced the number of regular employees to only a handful. When the two experts retired so close to each other, the plant literally shut down for weeks because, in effect, no one else knew how to "turn the lights on." The technical fog ended up costing the company millions of dollars.

If you cannot see through the technical fog, you cannot inventory and manage your unique technical capacity, and that is why you can't manage your talent risk well right now. Remember, talent risk is the gap in your current technical/professional capacity when compared to your expected three- to thirty-six-month resource demands.

To understand your technical capacity, you've got to be able to methodically get through that technical fog with a high degree of rigor and specificity. Hand waving or generalities will not do. You must be able to gather the data *on what each person actually knows how to do* so that you can ensure you'll have sufficient clarity, consistency, and capacity in the future.

> **You must be able to gather the data *on what each person actually knows how to do* so that you can ensure you'll have sufficient clarity, consistency, and capacity in the future."**

We often come across homegrown attempts at lifting the technical fog. We see spreadsheets, documents, and programs clients have created such as skills inventories, internal wikis, knowledge bases, heat maps, communities of practice, or fellows' programs.

If any of these talent risk efforts do lift the technical fog, they don't do so fully, measurably, or consistently, and they certainly don't go as far as the solution I will show in the next chapter. Still, the creative, homegrown attempts are evidence that the need is there.

Findings of the 2016 i4cp talent risk study showed the need is there as well. The study revealed there's no collective understanding of *what* talent risk data businesses should be gathering and measuring; no single metric was being regularly tracked by even half of the organizations. Only a third of businesses were measuring their current technical capacity. Of those not measuring technical capacity, seven out of ten executives either want this data but "can't find a feasible way to get at it" or are "just hoping for best."[12] They can't get through the technical fog.

But benefits await those who do lift the technical fog and use the

---

12 "Preliminary Results: Talent Risk Management Survey," Institute for Corporate Productivity, March 2016.

data to reduce their risk: Study analysts found the practice of assessing, identifying, and mitigating talent risk in critical technical positions correlated highly to high-performing organizations.[13]

DON'T SETTLE
FOR HALFWAY SOLUTIONS

There are some inherent problems with the homegrown solutions that we've seen. Since you likely have one or more of these solutions, I'll give you a few issues to monitor.

- If the "experts" are self-selected, you run the risk of spreading bad ideas like a virus.

- If more than one person is considered the expert, you run the risk of inconsistency.

- If you have multiple people trying to assess and solve the talent problem with no way to integrate their data or learnings, you will end up wasting the valuable time of your busiest people with no ongoing results to show for it.

- If you rely on job shadowing, it takes at least twice as long and is often frustrating.

- If a knowledge base is the solution, you run the risk that it is too shallow, out of date, or rarely used. And there is no way to measure outcomes.

- If you have individual heat maps, you run the risk of inconsistently assessing the degree of risk outside of any one team, leading to a lack of alignment and unclear priorities.

- If you have a college of experts or a fellows' program, you run the risk of their work being out of touch with the front line, or of the front line never getting access to their work in the first place.

---

13 Ibid.

The need includes going further than simply the ability to lift the technical fog. As a leader, you must be able to lift it when and where you want. You need to be able to zoom in right down to that granular level of what a specific team or individual worker can do.

Access to talent risk data needs to function like Google Earth (shown in the following table). When you open Google Earth, you're looking at the whole earth. This is akin to an executive presenting his or her strategy and big picture. Then, you find that with a simple click, you can zero in on your continent, then your country, state, and city. These views are like working down an org chart from the SVP level to the groups of technical workers within product teams. These levels of workers are all lined up to execute the strategy presented at the global level.

This is pretty cool. Google Earth has just brought you down to a map of your city, and your talent risk data has just helped you zero in on the critical teams required to execute your strategy. Then, just when you think there is no way you're going to get more detail in Google Earth, you break through to your neighborhood and then the street corner in front of your home, where you can see a crack in the sidewalk or a blade of grass. Fantastic! Talent risk data needs to zero in on technical workers in the same way. Each click should bring visibility to your unique technical workers by name, listing what each of them does. Finally, it should give you a detailed explanation of how and why they work.

Then, depending on the business decisions you're making at any moment, you should be able to zoom in and out with your talent risk data. You should be able to break through the technical fog between knowing a person's job title and knowing what they do for you at the most technical level, and zoom back up once you've ensured the risk is known and the biggest concerns are addressed.

Google Earth	Talent Risk Data
View of the world	Strategy and the big picture
View of the continents	SVP level
View of the countries	Divisional business unit heads
View of the states and cities	Product teams
Neighborhoods	Groups of technical workers within product teams
HERE'S WHERE YOU LIFT THE TECHNICAL FOG	
Streets	Unique technical experts
Homes	List of what each technical worker does (tasks)
Fire hydrant, blade of grass, front door	Detailed explanation of their work at the level of the right keystrokes or correct turns of a wrench.

Until now, most executives surely felt that getting data this granular was untenable or that the process to get there would collapse under its own weight and complexity. There is work involved in getting the data for sure, but it has to be quick and clear to be useful. You need to be able to lift the technical fog in a way that's practical, making real progress in a matter of hours or days, not weeks or months.

HOW DO I KNOW I'VE DONE IT?
WHAT "GOOD" LOOKS LIKE

How do you know you're lifting the technical fog? Going back to our Google Earth analogy, let's look at how this plays out at five different levels of your organization:

Board Level

As board members, you'll know you've lifted the technical fog when the CEO or president can provide you with a basic analysis of the technical capacity required to staff his or her strategic initiatives. Don't settle for "we're tapping into a pool of engineering talent in Zagreb." Seeing through the fog should mean an executive can use plain language to talk about the ten to thirty unique technical domains that, for each new initiative, link the current state of technology to the future state. Given the war on talent, finding new people to execute a strategy is plenty difficult; but in general, most organizations know how to do that. Repurposing a finite pool of existing technical people who can keep the legacy systems afloat while being pulled onto new projects is much trickier. Expect to see data that shows that talent risk analysis has been done and proper steps are being taken to manage it.

Executive Level

As executives, you will know you've lifted the technical fog when you can expect an updated inventory of all your critical technical talent that's accurate to within a month of the most recent organizational change. You're able to speak to the CEO or to the board about your plan for ensuring that your demographic profile is not going to crush your productivity or your competitive advantage. You'll be able to make decisions about head count allocation or reallocation with confidence that you're not going to do more harm than good. You'll be poised to respond to mergers, acquisitions, competitive threats, and other market forces because you know exactly where your technical talent is deployed, who is leading the technical charge, and where you face gaps that could be game changers.

Middle Management

Mid-level managers will know you've lifted the technical fog when you're confident that your most valued technical people are deployed to the most critical tasks nearly all the time. You will be able to report to your executives, with a high degree of confidence, that consistency and efficiency are tuned to the right level of rigor. When faced with a coming change, you'll be able to do scenario planning before formally announcing a reorganization so your people have confidence that you're making informed decisions. When leveling workloads between locations globally, you'll be able to guide the peer leaders toward clear role definitions and ensure they're ready to quickly troubleshoot any issues. When you hear of a critical retirement, it will be because you got invited to the party, not to the war room to figure out what can be done to handle the impending crisis.

Frontline Managers

Frontline managers will know you've lifted the technical fog because every member of your team will be working to their highest value and you'll have backups to cover all critical tasks. No longer will you have bottlenecks on your team that are the result of having no idea what one person does. You'll be able to explain your level of talent risk to your middle manager (down to the task level) so that if head count needs to be added or cut, you'll be able to clearly show the impact on your risk profile.

You'll retain your best people longer, because they'll see a career path that is technically interesting, and they'll have confidence that you as their leader can get them there. When you onboard a new employee or contractor, you'll be able to tell them exactly what they must learn to do to add value to the team. This will make them productive and happy in half the time it used to take. When you are faced with change such as a reorganization or a new system rollout, you'll be able to quickly figure out new roles and level new workloads with an eye toward reducing the inherent risk in change.

Outsource Partners

Outsource partners will know you've lifted the technical fog when they get a requirements document for the staff they are to provide along with the contract for deliverables and budgets. They'll use the clear description of standard skills and knowledge to ensure they are prepared to meet or exceed expectations routinely. When they have turnover, they'll refer to the requirements documentation to train a replacement. When their client is unhappy, they'll bring out the requirements document to clarify expectations and prepare to do better. They'll be more likely to have stability in their staffs and to make a profit, so they're more likely to negotiate lower costs when that is required.

Technical Workers

Technical workers will know you've lifted the technical fog because they will be able to answer the basic questions that everyone wants to be able to answer: What areas of technical expertise are required for my team to function and help execute the strategy? In which of these areas do I personally work? Am I setting the standard or following someone else's standard in each area? What areas should I be learning, and where am I already sufficiently consistent with the standard?

They'll also be part of a team that manages change head-on, assigning tasks to the right person, leveling workloads, reducing redundancy, and improving efficiency in part by ensuring an appropriate level of consistency. A side benefit of all that clarity is that they often really like their jobs and plan to stay a long time.

At this point you're probably thinking, *Steve, a solution that does all this is too good to be true.* No. It exists. It's been proven across numerous industries and all types of technical organizations. We lift the technical fog initially by creating lists of the technical expertise (knowledge silos) required to run any given group and then deciding who is the expert, who is doing work consistent with the expert's standard, who is learning, and who is *not* working in that area. After that, we analyze the risk that the organization will have sufficient people working in that area three to thirty-six months from now. Then, we help mitigate the risk through a variety of solutions.

The most extensive way we lift the technical fog is using a structured, on-the-job learning system called *knowledge transfer*. It's a groundbreaking, foundational shift in managing talent risk. In the process of figuring out what wisdom, tacit knowledge, and secret sauce must be transferred, we also figure out what should *not* be transferred. All of this depth of information is waiting on the other side of the technical fog for even the most complex role, regardless of industry. In the next chapter, I'll tell you all about how we do it.

DON'T SETTLE
FOR INADEQUATE INFORMATION

If you already have, or would like to have, some efforts underway to lift the technical fog in your organization, don't settle for inadequate information. The quality of the data is important, so let's look at the criteria that define if you've successfully lifted the fog. The data should provide support in all of these areas:

Specificity

- Zoom in to the individual contributor level. You should know the names of the people who are part of your risk profile.

- Agree on labels for their expertise. Everyone needs to be talking about the same risks.

- Clarify how many workers are involved. You need to be able to talk about capacity as part of your risk profile.

Relativity

- Show the sphere of influence for each chosen expert. Are they setting the technical standard for their team, their site, their region, or the world?

- Show how more than one expert around the world may be setting different standards and how they relate to each other. Otherwise, there is no hope for consistency.

- Align on language to describe the work so that redundancies and inefficiencies can be unearthed and mitigated.

Chunk-ability

- Deconstruct the blocks of knowledge into technical domains or silos that take a month to a year to learn so the expert can be clearly chosen and the silos can be discussed from the executive level to the front lines.

- List the skills and knowledge in consistent blocks of work (such as tasks that are teachable in about one hour) so they can be easily measured, staffed, and scheduled.

- Break the skills and tasks into steps and answers to questions that get at the wisdom, tacit knowledge, and secret sauce of the chosen experts. (I'll show how in the next chapter.)

Accessibility

- Gather the talent risk data in hours or days for a given expertise. It can't take too long or be too difficult for busy technical experts to participate.

- Scale the solution from 1 person to 1,000 people or more.

- Update the data regularly by spreading the workload between managers, experts, and others.

- Count the number of technical domains, experts, and capacity of workers per domain.

- Tally the cost of a mistake in each silo so that risk and priority are based on real impact.

(Continued . . .)

- Test the speed with which employees can learn a new skill or knowledge set and be prepared to go to work.

- Monitor risk reduction over time.

Predictability
- Keep the data current so it accounts for changes in team members and knowledge domains in relation to business goals.

- Standardize units of measure so that comparisons can be made between teams and predictions can be set for risk reduction timetables.

Usability
- Align with leaders at all levels around risk and priority for mitigating the risks.

- Conduct scenario planning using the data before a big reorganization.

- Level workloads and assign resources to ensure a ready workforce three to thirty-six months out.

CHAPTER 5

Assessing the Risks

Maria, a newly hired director, took over a team of technical writers, and she knew from the start that she was in for a challenge. Half the team was in India in one office, and the other half worked out of their homes spread across New England. She was based in the Boston office, and while she wasn't new to the company, she was new to managing technical writers and definitely new to this team.

The team's reputation was spotty, and there was a mandate to migrate from their old model for managing the documentation work-flow to a new one that would be more efficient and less expensive. The team in India needed to work consistently with the team in the US so work could be passed back and forth without regard for location. The team in India was made up of capable writers led by a solid manager, and they were ready to be put to work. Up to the time Maria was hired, they hadn't been fully utilized because there was no clear way to train them. In addition to the training issue, there was the matter of the new document management system that they needed to put to use.

Maria knew she needed to get clear about a few things quickly:

- Who are my people and what are they capable of doing today (from a technical writing, product knowledge, and a document process management perspective)?

- What is the status of the onboarding and utilization of the team in India?

- Who is leading the changeover from the old system to the new system, and what is the status?

- What is the gap between the way everyone is working now and the way they need to work going forward if we're to increase efficiencies and share work across the world?

- Where are the land mines in all this that might impact my team between now and when we stabilize on the new system?

These questions are just different ways of Maria asking, "What is my talent risk?" She needed answers and she needed more than a gut feeling to help her make quick decisions. She needed to know something about every person on her team so she could clearly understand the challenge and begin managing through it. She needed data.

Maria had some information to go on. She had a list of all her employees by name, tenure with the company, physical location, and job level. She had two managers—one for the US-based team and one for the team in India. She had made calls to introduce herself and get a sense of how things were going. All of this allowed her to zoom in to a certain extent, but then the technical fog began to obscure her ability to see clearly.

Once you've done the basics, as Maria had, the first phase of managing talent risk is lifting the technical fog. First, we want to gather data on each person's technical areas of expertise. Then, we can zoom in further using a tool that quickly uncovers both *explicit skills*—such as knowing the standard steps in a given process—as well as *implicit or tacit knowledge*. Tacit knowledge includes nuanced information such as why the process is done, what could go wrong, who needs to be involved, which rules must be followed, what to look and listen for, how to troubleshoot even the trickiest problems, and what outcomes or innovations should be shared with others in the organization.

Once you have lifted the fog, you can use the data in many ways to run your business. For example, Maria could see not only that all her experts were based in the US, but that there were several "camps" in her US-based team who had different ideas about how to implement the new technology. This was one of the reasons that they couldn't move forward faster—they hadn't agreed on, or been clearly told, what "going forward" actually meant. The team in India was somewhat helpless, because without a clear approach to the work, they could only pick up piecemeal projects rather than fully taking ownership of anything.

Along with her two managers, we helped Maria map a current state and future state picture of who would do what and whether they already knew how or would have to learn. In a matter of hours, Maria had the basic role clarity worked out—not just at the job title level but also at the functional/technical level. For her team, that included both process and product knowledge.

Maria could then turn her attention to ensuring her managers were fully utilizing all the head count to deliver high-quality output. The initial analysis of the data had quickly uncovered the names of her "experts" and showed who needed to be learning from each expert. It was time to zoom in further and figure out what each expert actually did day to day so she could replicate that approach across the rest of the team.

All this data could then be stored and updated over time to provide an at-a-glance picture of her global talent risk. When deadlines were at risk, quality was in question, workloads needed to be balanced, or it was time for a performance review, she could zoom in on any individual in her reporting structure long enough to get a quick update and then zoom back up to running the department. All this analysis of the risk was done in a matter of weeks, not months or years. If managed consistently across an enterprise, the process is quick and scalable. It works across cultures and demographics. Most importantly, it can be executed by extremely busy people with specialized knowledge who need an on-the-job solution because they can't take too much time away from doing their job to train others.

ZOOMING IN

A few years ago, I was working with a client that manufactures drug therapies out of blood plasma. While I was standing in the break room of the plant with the general manager, I overheard a conversation between the maintenance supervisor, one of his longtime mechanics (I'll call him Gus), and a new hire. This is roughly how it went:

> **Manager:** Gus, this is Jason, our new mechanic. Jason, as I mentioned, Gus here is a legend at this plant. For nearly forty years, he has kept the wheels turning and he knows every control panel, grease zirk, and cooling fan in the place. He can hear inaudible squeaks, anticipate warning lights before they turn on, and troubleshoot problems that start two buildings over. You want to be like Gus.
>
> Gus, I know we've been short-staffed lately. In fact, Jason here is our first new hire in nearly ten years, but I finally got management to give us some help. All I need you to do is show Jason the ropes. Could you "put him in your pocket" and let him follow you around for a while until he gets his feet under him?"
>
> **Gus:** Sorry, boss. I'm too busy. Nothing personal, Jason, but I have too much to do to keep this place from falling apart to give you much time.

And he started heading out the door. Now, my team had already been working with Gus, and we knew that one area of expertise he had was maintaining a huge and critical piece of equipment called a Lifealyzer. We had already written a plan that deconstructed Gus's role taking care of the Lifealyzer, so I thought I'd try an experiment.

> **Me:** Gus, hey, I know when we talked to you yesterday, you said you needed to get back to a big job on the Lifealyzer. You said you were going to change the gasket today.
>
> **Gus:** Yeah, that's right.
>
> **Me:** If you're up for it, Jason, your job today is to learn how to "change the gasket on the Lifealyzer," and by the end of the shift I want you to have learned a good chunk of Gus's forty years of experience related to this machine. You'll know you've learned something if you can answer five questions and sound just like Gus. Do you have a notepad? Here are the questions:
>
> 1. What are the steps in the process of changing the gasket, and why is each step important?
> 2. What are the most common mistakes newbies make when trying to change this gasket?
> 3. What do you look for, listen for, feel, and smell when changing the gasket?
> 4. How do you know if you're in over your head and need help?
> 5. How do you know you've done a quality job?
>
> **Jason:** So, I'm supposed to follow Gus and learn how to change the gasket. By the end of the shift, I need to get these answers out of him.
>
> **Me:** Yes. Gus, is that OK with you?

> **Gus:** Yeah, I can do that. I can start answering those questions on the walk over.

Gus went from walking away in a hurry, leaving his manager and his new colleague on the wrong side of the technical fog, to agreeing that he could help. His "knowledge" was suddenly visible, and it was a lot easier to imagine transferring it to Jason. Jason went from being a pain in Gus's side to taking charge of his own learning, starting with one task that needed to be done right away. The supervisor took one step toward reducing his talent risk.

DON'T SETTLE

STOP ASKING THE WRONG QUESTIONS AND START ASKING THE RIGHT ONES

The five questions I gave to Jason are part of a set of twenty questions that each expert is encouraged to use to help them organize their wisdom, experience, and tacit knowledge. Apprentices are encouraged to use the questions to keep the expert focused on the most important information and to validate for themselves and others how much they are learning.

THE KNOWLEDGE SILO MATRIX

Over the last twenty years, we've been figuring out the root cause of talent risk, and the Knowledge Silo Matrix (KSM) is the centerpiece of that effort. You might ask why it took so long to come up with what appear to be some common sense ways of thinking. I ask myself that question sometimes too. Basically, it took us twenty years to make it look this easy. We continually tested and honed the KSM (and other tools I will show you). We fixated on the idea that if we could "find simplicity on the far side of complexity," the tools would be easy to understand and use. They would be easy to maintain, readily quantifiable, scalable, and useful for anyone at any level of the organization and anywhere in the world who wants to analyze and solve the talent risk challenge. The Knowledge Silo Matrix (KSM) is a clear and simple tool to inventory the deep and narrow areas of expertise ("silos") that exist within any working team (see Figure 3).

The KSM also shows the capacity of the employees who are working in those silos relative to their role as experts/mentors, independent workers, and actively learning apprentices. In a matter of a few hours, a KSM can be developed for a roughly fifteen-person team *regardless* of type of job roles or complexity of technical knowledge.

> " The Knowledge Silo Matrix (KSM) is a clear and simple tool to inventory the deep and narrow areas of expertise ("silos") that exist within any working team."

On the KSM, a "silo" is a deep and narrow area of expertise usually consisting of twenty to one hundred skills and tasks that must be known for someone to work independently in that discipline. It usually takes a month to a year to learn these skills, so it is a big bucket of work. Knowledge silos typically include tools, processes, platforms, customers, physical locations, systems, and technologies that make up the work of the group. In Gus's case, one of his silos was clearly Lifealyzer maintenance. Changing the gasket was only one of the tasks/skills in this silo. And for Gus, the Lifealyzer was only one of more than two dozen silos for which he was the unique expert.[14]

---

14 I want to note that in using the term "silo," I am not advocating for increased specialization of workers. Being "siloed" is a pejorative in many organizations—and for good reason. I just find that calling them out in plain language is critical to truly understanding talent risk.

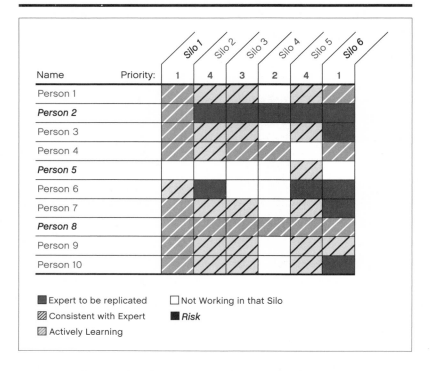

Figure 3. Sample Knowledge Silo Matrix. For a color version showing the employees who are purples, greens, and yellows, as well as areas of risk, see Color Insert 2.

I often use the analogy of building a house to explain silos. To build a house, you'll need work done in plumbing, roofing, siding, flooring, electrical, etc. You may even have subspecialties where the workers who do the framing are not skilled enough to do the finish carpentry, but both are "carpenters." Another way to help you think about silos is to picture your most valued employees and ask, "What are they the 'go-to person' for?" If Ranjit is the go-to person for lipid synthesis, that is probably a silo. If Christina is your go-to person for material testing, that is probably a silo, too.

By making a list of all your silos, you can break down the work of any team into the sum of its parts. And by labeling every silo, you begin to look at the *data* around your talent risk in a whole new way. You can have your plumber do your electrical work, but the risk to quality, schedules, safety, etc. would be higher and you'd want to be able to decide in advance if that level of risk is acceptable. Common sense would say that Jason, Gus's apprentice, could try to maintain the Lifealyzer before being fully prepared by Gus, but the risk would be higher.

Employee roles show up under each silo as a color. Purple on the KSM means that person is the *standard-bearer* and the *one we want to replicate* relative to this silo of knowledge. This is the "expert" or the "mentor" that everyone else will learn from. It is important to note that not just anyone can be purple. For example, some experts are "crazy geniuses," and replicating them would be a bad idea. And it is not better to have more than one purple because then you risk having too many standard setters. Purple is a job for the person who is asked to set the standard for the silo. Gus is a "purple" in the Lifealyzer silo.

A green box means the employee is *sufficiently* consistent with the standard set by the purple. Having a lot of green boxes on the KSM means that a team has a stable, competent workforce. Most people, like Jason, should aspire to be green.

A yellow box shows that the employee is pursuing the development of that skill. They're actively learning, and we call them the "apprentice." Someone could be marked yellow because he or she is new, because the silo is new, or because someone is being cross-trained or retrained. It is not a function of how old someone is or how long they've been with the company; and it is definitely not a bad thing to be marked yellow. Jason is a "yellow." Yellow means the person has a plan to get to green, and that is always a good thing.

White means the employee is not currently doing the work at this time. It doesn't mean they have never done it or couldn't do it if asked. It means that right now they are doing something else. For example, if Gus doesn't work on some other piece of equipment, he would be a "white" in that silo.

You can find a link to a sample KSM in Appendix I: Start Your Talent Risk Management Transformation in the Next 90 Minutes if you want to try your hand at completing a KSM for your own team.

TRANSLATING DATA INTO "RISKS"

Once you have the data in the KSM, you can immediately begin analyzing it and deciding what to do. In the sample KSM (shown in Figure 3 and Color Insert 2), you can see several potential risks. You might find it interesting to see if you can guess them before reading further.

- In Silo 1: Everyone is learning and no one is setting the standard. This will come up when a new system rollout such as an ERP is under way. The consultant hired to help is gone, and the employees haven't yet taken over completely.

- In Silo 4: The two apprentices have not yet become fully independent, and the expert in that silo is overloaded.

- In Silo 6: Too many experts means it is unlikely that a standard is clear, and consistency will be a problem. You don't want too many people setting the standard.

- Employee 2: This employee is expert in too many silos and has too much unique knowledge. If this employee also happens to be of retirement age, the risk is increased.

- Employee 5: This employee may be underutilized. It could be because she is "retired in place," or because she is a young engineer and her older colleagues have her doing busywork. It is also possible that this isn't a risk because she's a specialist and is needed in only one silo.

- Employee 8: This employee may be trying to learn too many new silos at one time. If the employee happens to be new to the company and/or right out of college, the risk might even be higher.

There is no algorithm that tells you how to interpret the data. That requires a conversation between managers and key stakeholders who know the "rest of the story." These are people, after all, and analyzing talent risk should take into account some of their humanity. We've just found that if you track their technical abilities and the roles they play, the softer side of people's backstory has a place to hang off the hard data in the matrix.

> " We've just found that if you track their technical abilities and the roles they play, the softer side of people's backstory has a place to hang off the hard data in the matrix."

The KSM gives them a framework and lexicon for the conversation that is consistent, quick, and clear. Chapter 8, Modeling the New Talent Risk Conversation, is all about this conversation.

In analyzing data from any given team, you'll find a lot of different nuances. For example, you'll find a silo where the risk is high but priority is low because the team is going to stop working in that silo soon and they can manage the risk between now and then. Or, you'll wonder how many people you can have in yellow before you should worry. If you have a lot of white, is that a problem? Having a lot of purple might sound good because that means you have a lot of "experts"—but what we really find is that isn't usually a good thing. We don't need a lot of people setting the standard, especially if consistency is critical to your success. For example, if you have three quality assurance teams in three locations around the world and they don't share purples in their common silos, they may have a lot of trouble working together.

Initially the KSM is always filled out for an intact team working under one manager or a functional team that works together in an "ecosystem" of interdependencies, such as a matrixed team or a project team. This is important because, while we often talk about the "experts" marked purple as the heart of the talent risk, the risk *mitigation* almost always involves everyone else. For example, if you have one expert marked purple in too many silos, you might ask someone marked green to take over setting and teaching the standard for one of the less-critical silos. That means the person marked green may need someone else to be marked yellow to learn in that same silo to provide additional capacity, and so on.

The KSM data provides a "talent risk profile" for a given team. By talent risk profile, I mean that stakeholders for that team's work—their bosses, peer teams, outsource partners, and the members of the team themselves—can see if they will or *will not* have enough skilled workers to get their job done in the next three to thirty-six months. Without a talent risk profile, all a manager's boss can say is, "How's your team doing?" All a manager can do is say "We're good" or "We're too busy."

But with a talent risk profile, real progress can be made. The 2016 i4cp talent risk survey found that conducting a "skill/knowledge gap analysis" ranked in the top three best practices for talent risk management—correlated to high-performing organizations both in importance and in effectiveness of addressing talent risk.[15] The KSM *is* a skill/knowledge gap analysis tool at its simplest and most relevant. In fact, several top behaviors in i4cp's checklist for successful talent risk management, published in their October 2016 report, reflect outputs of the KSM, including "Maintain a record of workers who possess skills and/or key knowledge required of each critical (or strategic) role" and "Identify and empower internal experts as arbiters of setting standards where consistency is a business imperative."[16]

---

15 "Talent Risk," survey results presentation by the Institute for Corporate Productivity, April 2016.
16 "Talent Risk Management: An i4cp Report," Institute for Corporate Productivity, October 2016.

The KSM provides this clarity on workers' critical knowledge, who the experts setting standards are, and where an organization has gaps.

Of course, analyzing talent risk with data starts with getting clean, consistent data and then keeping it current. We've found that the hard part of facilitating the data gathering and interpretation of the KSM exercise is not in picking the silos or the purples for one team. Many managers can do this on their own, and we've included instructions in Appendix I.

The tricky part comes when two or more managers try to share their data with each other and get "aligned." Remember, we want executives to be able to zoom in on the talent data for critical knowledge silos and be able to ask direct questions about whether the risk will be managed. If they zoom in, they need to trust that purple, green, yellow, white, and red all mean the same thing no matter where they are looking. And they need to know that priorities have been set according to a common logic. Those needs, by the way, are reflected in another best practice named in the checklist of i4cp's talent risk management report: "Have a common internal methodology and terminology for analyzing, prioritizing, and mitigating talent risk."[17] It turns out that simplicity on the far side of complexity requires a bit of disciplined work. Alignment on a common and precisely defined framework and lexicon across the enterprise is absolutely critical to making and keeping the data valuable over time.

---

17 "Talent Risk Management: An i4cp Report," Institute for Corporate Productivity, October 2016.

CHAPTER 6

Aligning Priorities

SARAH, AN IT DIRECTOR, HAD ONLY STARTED HER JOB WITH A MAJOR insurance company a few weeks earlier and had been working to familiarize herself with her new organization. She had one peer (Mateo) in her department, and between the two of them there were ten managers and seventy-plus employees and contractors. The department was split down the middle, with her team designing and building solutions, and her peer running support and maintenance of the solutions. As a result, they shared many areas of expertise and often shared team members between the two sides of the house.

Sarah had heard rumblings that this organizational structure had some good points, but it left too much room for the structure to take advantage of a few key people—and that had created bottlenecks and some turf wars. She had considered pushing for a reorganization to shake things up and clarify roles because that was what she'd done in the past. Mateo said that they had just put all seventy-plus members of their organization into KSMs (we call this a KSMx), and they agreed to see if they could sort out the challenges together using the data to guide and align them and their managers.

PRESENTING A TEAM'S RISKS

After gathering KSM data for each team, senior leaders like Sarah and Mateo can compare and analyze all the KSMs for their various teams at the same time by participating in a "KSMx alignment exercise." This meeting is attended by the senior leaders (often the Director and/or VP) plus all his or her direct reports—in this case, their ten managers. Each manager owns a KSM that represents seven to twenty people, including a combination of employees and contractors. The managers are prepared to present their matrices in no more than five minutes each. They stand with their matrix visible to everyone and they say—

- These are my silos across the top . . .

- These are the people I work with on the left . . .

- These are my risks (marked red) . . .

- These are my priorities for risk reduction . . .

Since everyone in the room (or on the phone) already reports in to the same leadership, it is easy to move quickly. The conversation focuses on risk and priority. A manager may introduce any number of these risks regarding their critical silos:

- I have one employee who is purple in too many critical silos and is also of retirement age.

- Two of my greens are getting bored and I must find them something else or they'll move on.

- I rely heavily on a purple who reports to another manager and is overloaded.

- We have to add two new silos this quarter to prepare for the new strategy, and those silos are currently all white.

- I'm personally still purple or green in too many silos and don't have time to do the management work required of me.

- One of my recent hires is still yellow long after his plan says he should be green. He is failing and I'm going to have to see about moving or firing him.

- The purple for one of our most critical silos is a contractor living in another country, and I'm not sure I can continue to count on him.

Once the risks are clear, a manager can present the priorities. He or she lays out the risks they're going to fix first so their boss and peers can agree or disagree with them on the priorities they've set.

A JURY OF YOUR PEERS— HECKLING FOR ALIGNMENT

In Sarah and Mateo's alignment meeting, one manager presented her KSM and laid out her priorities for her team. Her analysis made great sense to everyone except for one big problem. She herself was purple in almost every silo and she hadn't marked herself as "at risk." When one of her peers questioned her, she said, "Oh, I'm not at risk. I'm good . . ." In other words, she proved she had a real blind spot for herself. No one is "good" when they have so much unique knowledge, because the business would be at risk if she could not come to work one day. Alignment (and a better analysis of the risk) came in the form of a simple question from a peer.

In another presentation during the same meeting, a manager presented a KSM that was absolutely covered in red. He saw risk everywhere. Why was his team at such risk when the others seemed more on track? A few quick questions from his peers revealed the issue. It wasn't the team. It was how the manager was interpreting risk relative to the other managers. A brief conversation and the examples of how the other five managers looked at risk helped him recalibrate. Again, another alignment.

And when one employee showed up on five different matrices,

indicating that she was working for five different managers (even though technically she had only one boss), Sarah could say, "No wonder she's exhausted. You *all* think she works for you!"

Here's how the KSMx Alignment Exercise works. During a manager's five-minute presentation, the other managers study the KSM being presented. They will probably notice some issues like the ones I just described. Once the manager finishes presenting, his or her peers spend five minutes asking some of their own questions. I like to think of this as friendly "heckling."

- How come one of *my* employees is on *your* matrix? No wonder she's tired.

- Several of your silos were reorganized and handed to my team six months ago. Why are they still on your matrix?

- You show a purple in a silo that is in common/shared between our two teams, and I also have a purple in that silo on my team. No wonder they're butting heads.

- Your new hire appears to be yellow in everything. Is that practical? Is there a risk of the employee feeling overwhelmed?

- You have only one purple and no greens or yellows in a silo, yet it isn't marked red. Why is there no risk there?

- You have too many silos or people marked red. I think you're overdoing it.

- You have far too few silos or people marked red. I think you're being too conservative.

- I think your priorities are off and here's why.

Now, after only ten minutes (five minutes for presenting and five for listening), the manager who owns the KSM can take the feedback and either agree to take immediate action or at least agree to discuss the issue further. Here are some actions items they might take:

- Discuss a shared purple's capacity with his or her actual manager to level the workload.

- Mark herself red and begin reducing reliance on herself.

- Plan to stop doing work in a silo that is no longer part of his charter.

- Flip one of her purples to white so the wrong "expert" stops butting heads with the purple you want setting the standards.

- Flip some of a new hire's silos from yellow to white to reduce him or her from being overwhelmed.

The directors and/or VPs attending the alignment meeting are often silent the entire time because the work is being done by the managers. They watch for any disconnects that are not resolved on the spot, and they're ready to settle any disputes if needed. There is a certain logic that prevails, and they're often able to just let the process happen. Executives who like to give their leaders a lot of room to be self-directed love it because the decisions are being made at the right level and there is no doubt the decisions are being made consistently. After the meeting, the executive can expect from each leader a quick summary of action items that will be resolved in the coming weeks so that real progress can be seen by the time they get together again to realign. Color Insert 3 shows the results from a KSMx alignment meeting.

GETTING ALIGNMENT

Working with a client recently, we had leaders from nine different teams representing more than 190 employees and contractors. They all knew each other well and had been working together for years. Collectively, these managers led teams that audit major industrial complexes for everything from back-office paperwork to frontline safety. Their work is extremely technical and has enormous implications for the effective operation of their client sites. They had multiple goals to address. They were preparing for a heavy loss of unique technical talent through upcoming retirements. They wanted to increase efficiencies, improve the customer experience, and speed up cross-training so they could level workloads. And they had a remit from their board to do more work with fewer people in the coming year.

Each manager came to the alignment conversation with the KSM representing his or her team. Each KSM showed a combination of experts with decades of experience who interact with their clients for different reasons and at different times. Their trouble with alignment appeared in several areas. For example, they found that they had as many as twenty-one different knowledge silos where there was overlap between all twelve teams (highlighting the need for ownership of the standard and role clarity between teams). In each of those knowledge silos, there were as many as ten different people who were considered an expert, and each had a different way of conducting the work. Some leaders present were reluctant to imagine getting all those experts lined up under one standard (clarifying priorities). As each manager presented his KSM, there were disagreements on what it meant to be green (common lexicon) and which silos or people would be colored red (clarifying levels of acceptable risk). The lack of alignment threatened to derail the talent conversation.

THE FOUR AREAS OF ALIGNMENT

A KSMx exercise will only work if everyone is on the same page when it comes to four key areas: lexicon, ownership, acceptable risk, and priorities. To manage talent risk evenly across the division, leaders need to be aligned in all four areas.

Below are some questions we asked to ensure their leaders were working with a common baseline and that they were prepared to present their own talent risks in a way that made sense to the stakeholders in the room.

Alignment around a Common Lexicon

- What does "risk" mean for a given knowledge silo?

- How do you know who is the "expert"?

- What does it mean to be "apprenticed/actively learning"?

- What does "sufficiently consistent" mean?

Alignment around Ownership of Talent and Role Definition

- When you pass technical work to an outsource partner, do you pass responsibility to set the standard for the work? In other words, do you *outsource purple*?

- If three peer organizations all work in the same knowledge silos, who sets the standard for process and quality? How do you *pick the purple*?

- Once chosen, should the expert for a knowledge silo set the standard for her team, division, region, or for the world? Do you *share a purple globally*?

- When is it OK or even required to share an expert between teams for the sake of consistency? Should the purple *drive a common standard* outside his or her own team?

- If an expert is pulled from one project or team to another, what happens to his role on the former team? Does he continue to serve as expert or does he hand it off to someone else? When does a purple *stop being purple*?

Alignment Around Levels of Acceptable Risk

- If an executive pulls an expert from a legacy team to be part of a next-generation team, should there be any discussion about implications to the legacy team's ability to get their jobs done? What if the purple is needed elsewhere?

- How much core technical knowledge is OK to be maintained by an outsource partner? Is it OK to *outsource your purple*?

- Is it OK to have one person as the single point of failure for any knowledge silo?

- What is an acceptable cost of a mistake made by a worker who is not yet green on the KSM and not sufficiently consistent with the expert? What is the cost of *not knowing*?

Alignment on the Priorities

- Which knowledge silos must have a greater focus on consistency right away?

- Which knowledge silos get assigned the limited resources available?

- Which knowledge silos have resources removed to create greater focus on the highest risks?

- Which knowledge silos should be chosen to implement knowledge transfer?

By achieving alignment between leaders in these four areas, we laid the groundwork for our new talent risk management (TRM) conversation.

In the example of the auditors above, the disconnects and lack of alignment had been a real challenge; but with the KSMs' common lexicon and framework, the managers were able to resolve some issues on the spot and table others for further review. And they got to these decisions quickly: They conducted the first pass of alignment for nine teams and more than 190 people in just under two hours. As is common, each manager could present his KSM in about five minutes, with another five for discussion. In that short time, a decades-old problem was deconstructed into manageable challenges on which they could take *action*. They were ready to mitigate their prioritized talent risks.

CHAPTER 7

Mitigating Talent Risk by Transferring Knowledge

DO YOU REMEMBER SIMON, THE "SUGAR GUY" FROM CHAPTER 2?
He's the UK-based expert at a global confectionary company who picks the sugar for the next chocolate or biscuit product as it is in development. When we first met him, he was firmly hidden behind the technical fog. He had been known mainly as the go-to guy for glucose syrups—sugar—for nearly thirty years, and he was ready to retire. No one truly understood what he did every day, but when he gave thirty days' notice of his retirement, his manager and members of his team did know that it was a big deal to lose him, and someone would need to be trained to take over.

My team was tasked with finding out exactly what Simon did so we could transfer his knowledge in a hurry. Within a few hours of interviewing him, we learned that his job was nearly as exciting as James Bond's 007. His work involved deflecting potential corporate espionage, sniffing out falsehoods from vendors who were trying to secure his business unscrupulously, managing internal political battles between product groups, applying "genetically modified" requirements for local markets, and oh, by the way, choosing the glucose syrup for each new product, with disparate variables including taste, consistency, global availability, and cost. Simon's secret sauce was truly unique, and his company was worried.

Simon's company could have chosen several routes to mitigate the risk associated with his retirement. In my firm, we're knowledge transfer experts, so we'll focus this chapter on knowledge transfer as the one solution that works especially well for technical experts like Simon.

We have found over the past twenty years that a structured approach to knowledge transfer is routinely overlooked as a solution to mitigating talent risks. This is likely because few leaders have any idea it is even possible to take an expert like Simon and measurably replicate his skills. Or, they assume knowledge transfer is happening informally and that is the best they can expect. Finally, while I think there is plenty of agreement at the executive level on the need to replicate top talent, there is little alignment on how and when to prioritize (and allocate budget for) knowledge transfer relative to any number of other potential areas of focus.

Structured, measurable knowledge transfer is more than simply job shadowing and on-the-job training. It starts with gathering detailed data on the technical experts and their unique work—down to the keystroke level if needed. Then it is the planned movement of the right skills and information (including the secret sauce) at the right time to keep a workforce prepared, productive, innovative, and competitive. For Simon and his two apprentices, it meant thirty days to get thirty years of experience broken down into manageable tasks, transferred, and tested so there would be no break in continuity for the company once he retired.

MAKING "ON-THE-JOB TRAINING" METHODICAL, MEASURABLE, AND QUICK

In the early 1990s, I was a new manager at Microsoft, and we were hiring as many as fifty people a week to our growing team at a time when the company had only about 5,000 employees globally. During this era, folks routinely worked seventy hours a week, and the pressure to make a mark on the industry was palpable. My product, Microsoft Word, had less than 30 percent market share. We were fighting to beat the market leader, WordPerfect, and we were definitely the underdogs. Windows 3 had just shipped and DOS was just beginning to fade away.

I started thinking about the concept of how people learn at work—mainly out of pure frustration. I was a new hire, and so were many members of my rapidly growing team. We were all trying to get up to speed and were in learning mode *all* the time. Guess who we were learning from? The incredibly smart software developers among us. Now, these folks were nice enough; and if we caught them at precisely the right time, they'd answer our questions. But I swear, when they talked, I couldn't understand a thing they said. In the course of explaining themselves, they made assumptions about what I already knew. They referenced out-of-date documentation. They clicked around on their own computer screens to show me examples of what they meant with little context. They drew incomprehensible images on white boards using jargon that could have been ancient Greek, for all I knew. It was a fantastic time and place to be at Microsoft in many, many ways; but learning from these engineers was just too hard, time consuming, and frustrating—not only for my team, but for the engineers as well. From my point of view, we had a product to ship and a lot of people who didn't know what they were doing. We didn't have time to just "figure it all out."

So I came up with a plan to teach the experts how to be teachers so they could teach the rest of us how to do our jobs. I worked up a "train the trainer" program that a few people sat through. When it was over, they told me something that changed how I looked at the problem. They said, "Steve, I might stand up in a classroom and teach a class once a month, but I spend a couple of hours almost every day trying to explain what I do to people standing right here at my desk. Can you help me figure out how to teach in real time, on the job, rather than in the classroom?"

That sparked a whole new way of thinking for me that wasn't a new way of thinking at all. The idea of coworkers teaching or mentoring one another other while at work is nothing new. Apprenticeships have always been used to pass on trades from generation to generation. When life moved at a slower pace and jobs required less fast-changing, specialized knowledge, this system sufficed. Today, in most cases, it doesn't. For example, apprenticeships that rely on "job shadowing" don't move fast enough and don't scale well when your workforce is spread across the globe. But even with this new dynamic, one thing hasn't changed. Regardless of job role or industry, people still learn most of what it takes to do their job from their more experienced coworkers.

A study by the Center for Workforce Development proves the point. It says that people learn about 70 percent of their job skills by going to work and interacting with the more experienced people around them, regardless of how much formal training they have.[18] Think about your own career and a time when you've been asked to take on new responsibilities. What did you do? Chances are you combined reading, observing, researching, and studying, but you also had to learn from your more experienced peers.

While the apprenticeship model had been used for centuries, our situation at Microsoft felt unique. On the Microsoft Word team, our "technical experts" were really smart engineers who were *terrible* at explaining themselves. They were also under unbelievable time constraints. They were already overworked and 100 percent too busy to spend much time explaining themselves. And they were highly analytical engineers for the most part, so let's just say that communication and human interaction were not their strong suit. Being a young

---

18 Morgan McCall, Michael M. Lombardo, and Robert A. Eichinger, "70:20:10 Report," Center for Creative Leadership, 1988.

and largely male population hopped up on Mountain Dew and testosterone didn't make it any easier.

To help them methodically organize and transfer their knowledge faster, I needed to provide a structure that was logical, easy to use, and required as little time as possible. I had to get them to break their work down into manageable blocks of no more than an hour's time, show them the value of spending five minutes preparing a lesson plan of sorts, and then offer a way to deliver the content in a hurry, even if they weren't "good with people." Finally, I had to provide them a way to validate that their "apprentices" had *actually learned,* so the time they did spend transferring their knowledge was actually worth it.

I wrapped all of this in a plea to their selfish motivation. My message was that if they did a good job of transferring knowledge, they'd have real personal benefits. For example, they would only have to explain themselves one time. Their new colleagues could get to work in half the time, doing the work the "right" way. The newbies would ask fewer "stupid" questions and they would follow more of the unwritten rules. The experts would spend less time cleaning up the newbies' messes, and maybe everyone could have a little fun over the weekend rather than working to catch up. I didn't mention that their colleagues would not be as mad at them for being such lousy teachers. I didn't think the experts would care, but it meant the world to me. Reducing frustration for everyone was a great side benefit.

These experiences formed the foundation for our work in knowledge transfer. They eventually helped us develop a simple and clear methodology to replicate top technical talent on the job, mitigating talent risk along the way.

METHODICALLY TRANSFERRING KNOWLEDGE ON THE JOB

Here's how it works. The KSMx alignment exercise (in chapter 6) identifies the high-risk and high-priority areas of expertise (silos).

Executives can use this data to zoom in and out on their risks and pick those they want to fix right away. With that guidance, team leaders can request a "master plan" to transfer knowledge from the expert in that silo to any number of apprentices—anywhere in the world. The plan clarifies expectations and gives everyone something to track and measure so there is never any doubt that progress is being made to reduce the risks.

We call this plan the Skill Development Plan (SDP), and we create one for each high-risk, high-priority silo on the KSM. The Master SDP provides a measurable roadmap for all the unique skills an apprentice needs to learn to successfully work in the silo. It provides a clear list of each task they must be able to do, along with specific ways they can be "tested" to ensure they're competent. It also points at resources they can use to help them take responsibility for their own learning.

In Simon's case, the highest priority silo was "Glucose Syrups." Our initial job was to codify what he actually did every day, and we used the Skill Development Plan interview to deconstruct and outline that silo in about two hours. Before we dive into the creation of Simon's SDP, I want to set the stage a bit more and explain what we did to prepare him and his team for the exercise.

First off, it is important to note that Simon required what we call "emergency knowledge transfer" because we had only thirty days to replicate him before his retirement. In his defense, he said he'd been telling his bosses he was ready to retire for years, but they didn't believe him until he gave an actual date. Ideally, leaders would never have to do emergency knowledge transfer because they are mitigating the highest risks every day. That is certainly the case for most of our work; but in this case, the crisis was written in red on the calendar. Simon was only theirs for a mere month longer.

We got the call on a Friday and were ready to start work that next Monday. Our main contact was based in New Jersey but Simon lived in the UK, so everything I'm going to describe was conducted over the phone.

The Initial Meeting

First thing Monday morning, UK time, we were on the phone with Simon's manager, Janet. We listened to her explain a bit about Simon's role, his team makeup, and the timing of this challenge. With this information, we quickly created a Knowledge Silo Matrix with a list of eleven people in the left-hand column and fourteen silos across the top. Some of the people were already part of Simon's team, and a couple of them had to be "borrowed" from another group; even though they didn't currently report to Janet, they were the best candidates to apprentice to Simon's skills. Two team members were contractors who were based outside the UK. Collectively, this was Simon's "ecosystem," and we could use the matrix to plot a future without him. Some "greens" for each silo were quickly identified and there was talk of which greens would be asked to take over Simon's "purple" role as the standard-setter. Some yellows were identified to learn in the silos where the greens had to take on more of his work. Some people were flipped to white in lower-priority silos so they could focus on the higher-priority silos.

At the end of an hour, we had quickly gathered enough data to say that the highest risk, highest priority for Simon was definitely Glucose Syrups. Michael and Angie would be the two apprentices assigned. Michael was a veteran of the company and had worked with Simon for years, if at arm's length. Angie had only two years with the company so she had more catching up to do. It was determined that both would work side by side to learn the entire silo and then, after Simon left, they'd figure out how to divide up the actual work.

During this initial meeting with Janet, we also clarified exactly how many hours Simon would be available between that moment and his last day. "One month" as a time frame was quickly cut down by dentist appointments, a short vacation, a few tasks he needed to finish himself before he wrapped up, and the inevitable good-bye lunches and parties. When the dust settled on his schedule, we counted only forty-six hours available for him to work with Michael and Angie. It was a small window of opportunity so we couldn't waste a minute.

Our next meeting was later that same Monday morning with Simon, Janet, Michael, and Angie. We used that meeting to "kick off" the project and set the goal that by the time Simon left, Michael and Angie would be able to slide into his role and take over with as much clarity and confidence as possible. All of us knew that we couldn't replace Simon's thirty years in forty-six hours, but we could be sure that Michael and Angie *acted* like Simon in measurable ways. And Michael and Angie would *know what they didn't know*—what they might not have had time to learn—and get Simon's advice on how they could continue their education even once he was gone.

By the end of the kickoff, we had covered a lot of ground. We explained the process to everyone involved and focused all our attention on the Glucose Syrup silo. We clarified roles and laid down a clear project plan with dates and measurements. We talked about how we'd use the forty-six hours and how each one had to be protected from their regular work and from other fire drills because the time was so short. We all agreed it would have been better to start a year earlier, but we'd have to make the best of it. Janet agreed to be chief problem solver if anything threatened to get in the way.

We left the meeting with a clear plan, ready to start work the next day (Tuesday), and agreed on a formal status report that we'd fill out every couple of days to keep everyone up to date on progress.

Tuesday morning we were ready to write the Master SDP for the Glucose Syrups silo.

Creating a Skill Development Plan

The SDP was written in a few hours by facilitating a conversation with the expert marked purple—in this case, Simon. Since we were in a hurry, we agreed that Michael and Angie would listen in on the interview so they could help provoke Simon from their own point of view and they could begin learning by seeing the SDP take shape.

To write the plan, we literally said, "Simon, since you have been marked 'purple' and asked to set the standard for this silo, what is it you *do* that makes them think you're such an expert?" In my twenty years doing this, I've only heard versions of one answer to this question, and Simon was no exception. Basically, he said, *"I have no idea. I just do my job."*

We then asked him to help us figure it out. The dialogue with Simon went like this:

> **Facilitator:** Let's see if we can make a list of all the work you do in each product development cycle. For example, do you have to read any complex technical documents?
>
> **Simon:** Yes. I read and provide feedback on the glucose specification for each product.
>
> **Facilitator:** Is this something anyone with an appropriate degree in food sciences could read?
>
> **Simon:** No. Most of my current colleagues couldn't even read it.

Then a skill is added to the Skill column of the SDP: "Read and provide feedback on the Glucose Spec." Then the facilitator kept digging.

> **F:** Do you analyze anything?
>
> **S:** Yes, I analyze glucose syrup properties relative to the product requirements.
>
> **F:** Do you troubleshoot anything?
>
> **S:** Yes, I troubleshoot problems with collapsing sweet.
>
> **F:** Do you manage any relationships?
>
> **S:** Yes, I call and negotiate with Pierre on biscuit product requirements.
>
> **F:** Do you manage any other relationships?

S: Yes, I assess whether vendors are telling us the truth when they present their product line.

(Note: This one didn't come out this cleanly at first, as you might imagine; but once we started talking about managing relationships, it turned out they were a huge part of Simon's work. Michael and Angie were blown away because they had no idea.)

F: Do you test anything?

S: Of course, I conduct structured sensory evaluations of samples.

F: Do you monitor anything?

S: Yes, I monitor relative costs of glucose and sugars in all markets.

This is what the SDP started to look like for Simon:

Skill and Task	Sequence	Test Questions	Due Date	Actual Date	Resources
Silo: Glucose Syrups					
Read and interpret glucose specifications	1	1,2,3,4,18,19	May 1	May 1	Simon / Product Division
Assess required properties for glucose syrup	2	4,18,19,12,13	May 2	May 2	Simon / Product Division
Troubleshoot problems with collapsing sweet	5	1,2,3,4,5,7	May 8	May 9	Patrick / QA Division
Negotiate biscuit product requirements	7	1,4,18,19,14	May 19	May 21	Sophia / Legal
Conduct sensory evaluation of samples	8	3,4,5,19	May 21	May 21	Simon / Product Division
Monitor relative costs of glucose in all markets	6	3,4,5,19	May 12	May 12	www.costwatch.com
Assess supplier equipment capabilities for making samples	9	3,4,5,19	May 30	May 30	Specifications located at //internal site

Skill and Task	Sequence	Test Questions	Due Date	Actual Date	Resources
Assess regulatory requirements for a non-standard glucose	3	1,7,11,14,19	May 3	May 3	www.food.gov.uk/enforcement/regulation
Assess regulatory and genetically modified requirements for local markets	4	1,7,11,14,19	May 6	May 6	www.food.gov.uk/enforcement/regulation

Figure 4. Glucose Syrups Skill Development Plan

Notice that as each line is added to the SDP you can imagine taking a picture of the expert doing it. For example, I can imagine Simon on the phone calling to negotiate with Pierre on their biscuit product requirements. Conversely, if the verb at the beginning of each line was less clear—for example, *"Understand* relative costs of sugars by market"*—apprentices wouldn't know what they are supposed to *do* with the *understanding.* If you can imagine taking a picture of the expert doing it well, you can also imagine taking a picture of the new apprentice making a mess of it. If we put this clear task or skill in the SDP and methodically train the apprentices, we can reduce the risk of failing or even being inconsistent with the expert. That is one of the ways we know we're solving the problem.

**DON'T SETTLE
FOR UNCLEAR DEVELOPMENT PLANS**

Nothing on an SDP is academic. All of it is *doable* in the most practical sense. You'll never see a skill listed as "be familiar with . . ." or "have a background in . . ." because you could never say to an apprentice, "Today, I want you to go get a background in glucose syrups." That wouldn't make any sense. There are three basic rules for creating an SDP:

(Continued . . .)

1. Start with a verb.

2. Provide direction and role clarity. You can say, "Go do it."

3. Break skills into chunks so each skill can be explained in about an hour.

For example, I once interviewed an expert from a major shoe manufacturer who was training his apprentice to finish an invention for automating shoe manufacturing. As we tried to write the Skill Development Plan, he got frustrated. Our expert said, "I have to start with giving Kim [his apprentice] a master's degree in material science."

In response, I said, "If he had a master's degree in material science, what would you then have him *do*?"

He said, "I'd have him test the heat resistance capacity of a piece of fabric."

"Well," I said, "why don't we just teach him how to do that?" And we did.

Making Sure Skills are Measurable and Self-Driven

Once we had the Skill column filled out for the Glucose Syrup SDP, Michael and Angie had an answer to the age-old dilemma of every apprentice. Instead of "I don't know what I don't know," they now had a clear list of what they might not know. In this case, seventy-two tasks and skills collectively catalogued the work in the silo. This number fell right within the average for all silos, regardless of the kind of work being done. Each skill would be teachable in about an hour, so we also knew how much time we would require to cover them all. Right away, we knew that Simon's forty-six available hours would not be enough and we'd have to prioritize with the cost of a mistake in mind. Now we were ready to fill out the Test Question column and the Resources column of their plan to make it measurable and self-driven.

The Test Questions column is where we pick questions we want

Michael and Angie to be able to answer in order to sound like Simon. In addition to looking at their work products, this is how we measure whether they have learned. There are twenty questions to draw from, and the same twenty questions work for any topic no matter how creative, scientific, technical, cultural, global, relational, operational, or conditional. We use these questions to transfer knowledge on every topic imaginable. Below is a quick scenario to help you understand how they work.[19]

Simon, Angie, and Michael went through each line in the plan and picked a handful of test questions they wanted to cover when the time came to discuss that skill. Each line was a little different, so a different set of the twenty questions was in order. For them, it was like ordering a pizza. Angie might say, "I'd like to learn about questions 3, 6, and 7 for that skill, please." Michael might like a different list. Of course, Simon had an idea of what they ought to want to know, and he weighed in as well. At the end of the day, Michael and Angie knew that being able to answer these questions with what they learned from Simon was a clear metric to prove that they could take over.

For example, when it was time for Simon to teach the skill "*Assess whether vendors are telling us the truth when they present their product line*," here are the questions Michael and/or Angie chose, along with some sample answers to give a sense of the kind of information the questions elicited:

> **Question #2.** *What are the steps in the process (of doing this assessment), and why does each step matter?* Simon started with research, gave them questions to ask, and provided pointers on each type of vendor.

> **Question #3.** *What are the top three things that often go wrong when someone is learning this skill?* Simon told some war stories and gave them a good list of "dumb moves" to avoid.

---

19 You can get the full list at www.stevetrautman.com.

Question #6. *What is the potential cost of making a mistake?* Simon explained how picking the wrong vendor could disrupt the global supply chain and shut down production, potentially costing millions.

Question #18. *What do you look for, listen for, feel, or smell?* Simon talked over the kinds of "tells" that he'd experienced with various vendors who were trying to pull a fast one, so they weren't able to get away with it.

Next, they all worked to fill out the Resources column to catalogue the resources available to help Michael and Angie learn and ultimately work without Simon's help. For each line in the plan, they asked Simon to point them to the documents, samples, templates, training, and people that would be the most relevant and current resources to get them going on that task. In so doing, Simon also steered them clear of content and contacts that were *not* a good way to go.

By the end of the meeting on Tuesday morning, we had written the Master Skill Development Plan and were ready to map out the rest of the month, focusing on the most critical and relevant tasks and skills first. This is where the Sequence and Date columns come in.

When completing the Sequence column, you need to keep several factors in mind. For starters, Michael and Angie each needed to have their own customized plan. Michael had more experience, so he didn't need to learn everything that Angie did. There were times that both would not be available at the same time to learn from Simon. In some cases, the work was going to be split between them, so one or the other could skip a session. Finally, Simon had only forty-six hours, and there were seventy-two lines on his plan—so some content was not going to be covered in person. Their manager, Janet, returned for the meeting where we filled out the sequence column so she could weigh in from her perspective.

Last, we filled out the Date column. This is where we sketched the

COLOR INSERT 1
Talent risk management sits at the intersection of strategy, people, and risk.

STRATEGY

RISK

PEOPLE

COLOR INSERT 2
Sample Knowledge Silo Matrix (color version)

IDENTIFY RISK
Knowledge Silo Matrix

Name	Priority:	Silo 1	Silo 2	Silo 3	Silo 4	Silo 5	Silo 6
		1	4	3	2	4	1
Person 1							
Person 2							
Person 3							
Person 4							
Person 5							
Person 6							
Person 7							
Person 8							
Person 9							
Person 10							

■ Expert to be replicated   ☐ Not Working in that Silo
■ Consistent with Expert   ■ Risk
☐ Actively Learning

KSMx to determine risk and possible responses

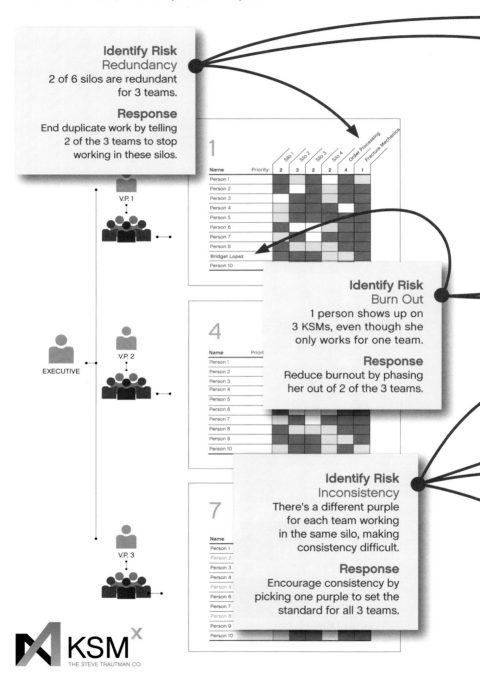

Identify Risk
Redundancy
2 of 6 silos are redundant for 3 teams.

Response
End duplicate work by telling 2 of the 3 teams to stop working in these silos.

Identify Risk
Burn Out
1 person shows up on 3 KSMs, even though she only works for one team.

Response
Reduce burnout by phasing her out of 2 of the 3 teams.

Identify Risk
Inconsistency
There's a different purple for each team working in the same silo, making consistency difficult.

Response
Encourage consistency by picking one purple to set the standard for all 3 teams.

EXECUTIVE

V.P. 1

V.P. 2

V.P. 3

KSM^X
THE STEVE TRAUTMAN CO.

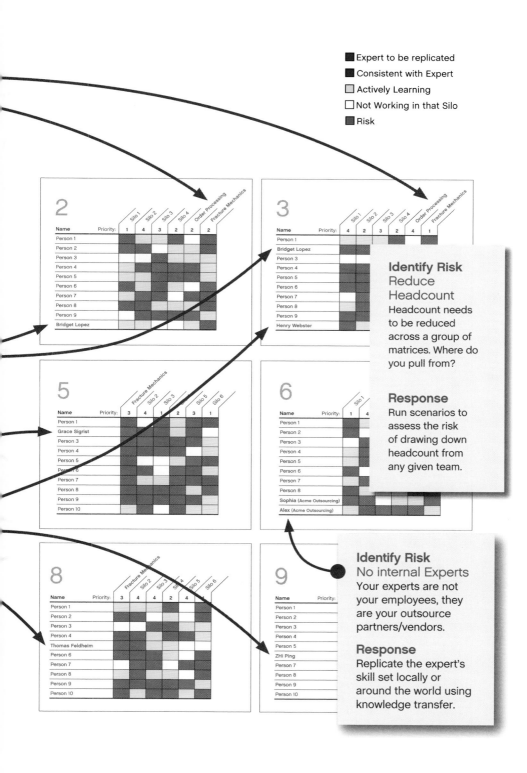

BEFORE: A partial image of a Knowledge Silo Matrix (KSM). KSM prior to knowledge transfer efforts.

Legend:
- ■ Expert to be replicated
- ■ Consistent with Expert
- ▨ Actively Learning
- □ Not Working in that Silo
- ■ Risk

Employees Names	Locations	General Ledger Silo	Inventory Silo	AP Silo	AR Silo	ProjectXXXXXX	XXXXXXXXXX
Silo Priorities		1	1	2	2	2	2
Employee 1 (Training Team)	East						
Employee 2 (Training Team)	East						
Employee 3 (Training Team)	East						
Employee 4 (Current ERP User)	Midwest						
Employee 5	Midwest						
Employee 6	Midwest						
Employee 7	Midwest						
Employee 8	Midwest						
Employee 9	Midwest						
Employee 10	Midwest						
Employee 11	Midwest						
Employee 12	Midwest						
Employee 13	Midwest						
Employee 14	Midwest						
Employee 15	Midwest						
Employee 16	Midwest						
Employee 17	Midwest						
Employee 18	Midwest						
Employee 19	Midwest						
Employee 20	Midwest						
Employee 21	Midwest						
Employee 22	Midwest						
Employee 23	Midwest						
Employee 24	Midwest						
Employee 25	Midwest						
Employee 26	Midwest						
Employee 27	Midwest						
Employee 28	Midwest						
Employee 29	Midwest						
Employee 30	Midwest						
Employee 31	Midwest						
Employee 32	Midwest						
Employee 33	Midwest						
Employee 34	Midwest						
Employee 35	Midwest						
Employee 36	Midwest						

BEFORE

AFTER: KSM showing how the Midwest plant's team reduced talent risk through their knowledge transfer efforts. The team switched from yellow "Actively Learning" to green "Consistent with Expert."

■ Expert to be replicated
■ Consistent with Expert
□ Actively Learning
□ Not Working in that Silo
■ Risk

Employees Names	Locations	General Ledger Silo	Inventory Silo	AP Silo	AR Silo	ProjectXXXXXX	XXXXXXXXX
Silo Priorities		1	1	2	2	2	2
Employee 1 (Training Team)	East						
Employee 2 (Training Team)	East						
Employee 3 (Training Team)	East						
Employee 4 (Current ERP User)	Midwest						
Employee 5	Midwest						
Employee 6	Midwest						
Employee 7	Midwest						
Employee 8	Midwest						
Employee 9	Midwest						
Employee 10	Midwest						
Employee 11	Midwest						
Employee 12	Midwest						
Employee 13	Midwest						
Employee 14	Midwest						
Employee 15	Midwest						
Employee 16	Midwest						
Employee 17	Midwest						
Employee 18	Midwest						
Employee 19	Midwest						
Employee 20	Midwest						
Employee 21	Midwest						
Employee 22	Midwest						
Employee 23	Midwest						
Employee 24	Midwest						
Employee 25	Midwest						
Employee 26	Midwest						
Employee 27	Midwest						
Employee 28	Midwest						
Employee 29	Midwest						
Employee 30	Midwest						
Employee 31	Midwest						
Employee 32	Midwest						
Employee 33	Midwest						
Employee 34	Midwest						
Employee 35	Midwest						
Employee 36	Midwest						

AFTER

BEFORE SCENARIO PLANNING: The initial KSM for the Midwest plant-based Primary Operations team. Employees 1 and 2 are experts taking early retirement.

Legend		Caster Scheduling	Caster Production	Bxxxx Applications	Bxxxx Production	Bxxxx Tracking	Bxxxx Physical Inventory	TXX Shipments	TXX Scheduling	TXX Production	TXX Order Processing	Handoffs
■ Expert to be replicated												
■ Consistent with Expert												
▢ Actively Learning												
☐ Not Working in that Silo												
■ Risk												

Employee Names	Locations											
Employee 1	Midwest Plant											
Employee 2	Midwest Plant											
Employee 3	Midwest Plant											
Employee 4	Midwest Plant											
Employee 5	Midwest Plant											
Employee 6	Midwest Plant											
Employee 7	Midwest Plant											
Employee 8	Midwest Plant											
Employee 9	Midwest Plant											
Employee 10	Midwest Plant											

AFTER SCENARIO PLANNING: A partial KSM of an early reorg scenario that presented too much risk and was eventually discarded. The desire had been to centralize support for Primary Operations functions of all plants with employees physically at the Midwest plant. Note the silos at risk.

These images show the Knowledge Silo Matrix's (KSM) usefulness for scenario planning of reorganizations and downsizing.

- Before reorg scenarios, the risk to the Midwest plant team shown in Color Insert 6 is manageable. The risk of departing Employees 1 & 2 could be mitigated by each apprentice completing, on average, 4 customized Skill Development Plans (SDPs)—a reasonable goal.

- Color Insert 7 shows an early reorg and downsizing scenario that was eventually discarded because it introduced too much risk.

  First, in addition to the two experts leaving, Employee 9 from the original team would be let go since he is not working in any of the current silos.

  Then, as part of a reorg, management wanted to centralize the primary operations for all the plants into one location. While all locations have a team for primary operations, the actual work in each plant is different. By moving operations to the Midwest, the Midwest team would be required to learn 30 additional silos with each apprentice completing, on average, 21 SDPs—an impractical goal that would take years to achieve.

Bxxxx Shipments	TXX Scheduling	TXX Production	TXX Order Processing	Caster Scheduling	Caster Production	Bxxxx Applications	Bxxxx Production	Bxxxx Tracking	Bxxxx Physical Inventory	Bxxxx Shipments	TXX Scheduling	TXX Production	TXX Order Processing	Caster Scheduling	Caster Production	Bxxxx Applications	Bxxxx Production	Bxxxx Tracking	Bxxxx Physical Inventory	Bxxxx Shipments	TXX Scheduling	TXX Production	TXX Order Processing
Coast Plant				Formerly at Mid-Atlantic Plant										Formerly at Southeast Plant									

SCENARIO

Initial KSM of software developer's writing team. Note the lack of experts in a majority of silos.

	Advanced Tech Writing				Authoring Tools			Dxxx				Product Knowledge									Project Leads		
	Single Source	Doc Design	Doc Usability Testing	Architecting Info Delivery	FrameMaker	RoboHelp	Wiki	Content Dev PT	Content Maintenance	Project Analysis	Content Design	Storage Management	Pxxxxx Pxxxx	Cloud Computing	Bxxx	Proxxxx	Acxxxx	IT Xxxxx	Network	Infrastructure	Project Estimation	Project Dxxx	Doc Plan
SILO PRIORITIES	2	1	1	1	3	2	3	3	3	2	1	3	3	1	2	1	1	3	3	3	2	1	2
Employee																							
Employee 1																							
Employee 2																							
Employee 3																							
Employee 4																							
Employee 5																							
Employee 6																							
Employee 7																							
Employee 8																							
Employee 9																							
Employee 10																							
Employee 11																							

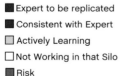

■ Expert to be replicated
■ Consistent with Expert
☐ Actively Learning
☐ Not Working in that Silo
■ Risk

basic flow of the month so we could do regular status check-ins. This column was critical to keeping the three of them moving. Since every topic was meaty and interesting, they could easily get bogged down—spending too much time on one topic rather than marching through the plan on schedule. We recommended that they literally set a timer at the outset of every knowledge-transfer session so they could stay on track.

As a reminder, we don't usually work with emergency knowledge transfer. If this team had been assembled without the harsh deadline imposed by Simon's impending departure, they could have spread these sessions out over a year or more.

During the next three weeks, Simon met regularly with Michael and Angie in one-hour sessions where they'd agree on the line in the plan to be taught, confirm which test questions he was going to cover, and confirm which resources were relevant and useful. Then Simon would "teach to the test," after which Michael and Angie would paraphrase what they learned (by literally answering the test questions aloud) so Simon could confirm that they were on track.

Along the way, they provided quick status updates to Janet by simply showing her which lines in the plan were getting covered each day. Janet sat in on a few of the sessions to confirm that Michael and Angie were indeed answering the test questions and sounding more and more like Simon. This gave her confidence that they'd be able to take over. If they had *not* been able to answer the questions, she could have taken action and traded out apprentices as needed.

During Simon's last couple of days on the job, the team was able to use the SDP to confirm what they had *not* covered and do what we call a "lightning round." For every line in the plan that would not be taught in a one-hour knowledge transfer session, we had Simon spend five minutes ensuring the resource column was as complete as possible and talking through his best advice for how they could carry on with their training despite not having him available.

On Simon's last day, everyone was relieved, especially Simon. He knew he'd done all he could to prepare Michael and Angie to take over and that his legacy was intact. Janet had confidence that her team was well positioned to move forward, and, of course, Michael and Angie were ready to go to work. They were also already talking about using the same SDP to begin sharing what they'd learned with others so the team would never have a single point of failure like Simon again.

Planning for an Uncertain Future

Simon had an immediate, known skillset, and the company had a thirty-day window to identify and transfer his knowledge. The chief architect for a healthcare insurance company has the exact opposite situation. He has to prepare a team for anything that might come at them at some time in the future if and when technology disrupts their markets. That is a tall order. But the SDPs apply to both talent risk situations.

The architect was hired in with a seemingly impossible mission to *be the transformational force that changes the nature of healthcare.* His team of 200 solution, technology, systems, business, and integration architects will need to disrupt current thinking in healthcare and lead a digital transformation that changes the very business model on which the company operates.

He knows he is not building a team for a moment in the future when the transformation is "complete." He is training people how to think about the future and be ready for anything. The challenge will be to break all that vision down into actions that ordinary—albeit excellent—architects can execute quickly.

While he is preparing his team for the transformation, he has ongoing talent risks. The chief architect is—and should be—on the front end, pulling the team toward his vision. But as a counterbalance there needs to be a healthy tension with the technical leader who maintains the legacy systems, keeping a sufficient number of technical resources to maintain a standard of service. There is always a desire to pull experts off the legacy systems to build the new team, and his counterpart will need a way to push back. They can both use the KSM and the SDPs to facilitate conversations, like the risks of taking a person off legacy now versus taking them when the team is stable enough the disruption has a *reasonably low* risk.

He and I talked about how the SDPs can help expedite the digital transformation at the tactical level. He can use them to clarify expectations for process and quality. He can use them to give feedback for anyone who is stuck in the old way of doing things and to onboard new people into their process. It is all about getting the right team in place and having them be prepared to move faster with a clear and *measurable* path.

While I have extensive field-based evidence to prove that the process I've described here with Simon works, independent research now supports it too. The use of Skill Development Plans—and knowledge transfer overall—to mitigate talent risk was highly validated by the research findings of i4cp's talent risk survey. Here are several of my favorite data points.

First, like the results around the Knowledge Silo Matrix, i4cp researchers found that "skill development plans" ranked in the top five best practices for talent risk management—correlated to high-performing organizations both in importance and in effectiveness for addressing talent risk.[20] Second, "Having a process in place to ensure transfer of critical knowledge" and "Having individual development plans and accountability practices to ensure that the most critical talent gaps are closed" made the October 2016 report's checklist for excelling at talent risk management.[21] Third, measuring the amount of critical knowledge being transferred or cross-trained was cited as

---

20 "Talent Risk," survey results presentation by the Institute for Corporate Productivity, April 2016.
21 "Talent Risk Management: An i4cp Report," Institute for Corporate Productivity, October 2016.

a next-gen metric for assessing the effectiveness of a talent risk management program.[22] All great validation of what I've seen day in and
day out in the field.

As a final note on this chapter, I want to point out again that
Simon's story was unique because of the emergency created by his
short timeline. A more typical scenario would have had Janet, Simon,
Michael, and Angie included in an enterprise-wide talent risk assessment, which would be followed by routine knowledge transfer that
had been built into their everyday workload and embedded in the
routine business practices of their org. The conversations would have
been the same, the tools and processes would have been identical,
and the results would have been equally satisfying—but the cost to
the individuals and the organization would have been far less.

---

22 "Talent Risk," survey results presentation by the Institute for Corporate Productivity, April 2016.

CHAPTER 8

Modeling the New Talent Risk Conversation

THE CHRO HAS JUST MET WITH HER CORPORATE BOARD AND THEY'VE asked her a question she can't answer with any degree of confidence. They want to know what she is going to do to ensure her organization has enough technical people in place to take care of the combination of turnover and growth clearly on the horizon. They also want a talent plan to back up the strategic initiative the CEO has just presented. They don't want to get into the weeds on the topic, so she needs to explain her approach in simple terms they can understand.

A COO has a vision to usher in big technical and process advancements to help execute his company's business strategy. Implementing his vision requires reassigning some of his best people to a new task force, and these talented technical experts are already busy delivering important work. The COO wants to extract and repurpose these experts as quickly as possible, but it has caused a huge uproar among the team leaders who will have to live without them.

One of these experts is the bottleneck for a whole department. All decisions seem to require a conversation with her, and she's too busy to even show up to a meeting. Her boss and her peers know she's overloaded, but all they can do is talk about their frustrations. There seems to be no way there will ever be time to solve the problem. Oh, and she's already of retirement age and could choose to leave at any moment.

In the field, two seasoned experts are fighting a silent war over who will set the standard for how their technical work gets done. One is in Houston and the other is in New Delhi. Both have reason to believe they are right. They've tried to talk to each other and resolve their differences, but they keep getting stuck. It just seems easier to pretend the other isn't there and go about their business.

On the shop floor, a beloved longtime expert is revered for his vast experience and deep understanding of his job. Since he started thirty years ago, there have been a few (!) changes made that constitute the "new" way of doing things. The trouble is that this technical expert has been more than a little selective about how much of the "new" way he's chosen to adopt. Now that he's retiring, it is hard to sort out the good from the bad as he is asked to transfer his knowledge to the next generation before he goes.

In the Paris office, an IT team leader provides support for a collection of complex technologies, each one delivering what is believed to be a "mission critical" service to the organization. The trouble is that staff has been cut and the team can't possibly do it all anymore. Something has to give or there is a risk of failing where the cost of a mistake is millions of dollars. So far all his boss can say is, "Hold on. We'll figure something out."

To cut costs in North America, an outsource partner was selected to take over a broad variety of technical work. They even hired some of the technical experts who lost their jobs in the process and took over the lease on some of the space where these people worked. It was supposed to be seamless, but over time the experts found jobs in other firms, and the outsource partner began to fail at providing critical services. The client needs to renegotiate the outsourcing contract and reset service levels, but with all their experts gone, management doesn't really know what they're asking the outsource partner to do.

GETTING EVERYONE ON THE SAME PAGE

In every one of these examples is an opportunity to make well-informed decisions, and the stakeholders are eager to make them. What they lack is a framework for getting to the heart of the talent issue, identifying choices, and then calling a play. It isn't that they're not talking—in fact, they seem to be in an endless string of meetings—it's just that the discussion is not serving them well. They need a framework and vocabulary that bring data into a practical conversation. This will create a crucial leadership alignment around the concepts of technical ownership, guideposts for acceptable risk, and criteria for setting priorities.

No doubt the leaders are already talking about talent risk, but the results of these conversations are usually not very satisfying. Does this sound familiar? How are you doing talking about talent risk in your organization? You're probably asking questions like, *"What's the succession plan? How much of my workforce is retirement eligible? Why is Chris always a bottleneck on our projects? What is our ratio of employees to contractors? What's our attrition rate? What did the employee engagement survey say?"*

The trouble with these questions is that even when well executed, the answers are not very helpful. For instance, once you know that 40 percent of your workforce could retire at any time, what do you do? Hire younger people? How do you know that is going to make any difference at all? Identifying a key employee as a bottleneck is often stating the obvious, but then what? These talent management conversations are disappointing and frustrating.

I want you to be able to have a much more satisfying and productive conversation—one based in data that can quickly guide informed decisions.

You can't have the conversation until you establish that everyone is talking about the same thing. For example, just because the executive team has communicated the company's strategy doesn't mean your people understand it and its implications. So, first you have to validate their understanding by asking what I call the Big Picture Questions (see the following "Don't Settle" information). With these nine crucial questions about the big picture, you can ensure that your people truly grasp and can articulate how your strategy applies to their work. If they can answer the nine questions and sound like their boss and their peers, they "get the big picture." If they can't, you have some work to do in clarifying expectations.

The Big Picture Questions should eventually be answered by everyone—right down to the lab technician, the data analyst, and the receptionist. This is *not micromanagement*. It is a clear measure of being an effective leader. If your team can't answer these questions, you haven't done a good job of presenting your organization's strategy and you can't be surprised if the results are disappointing. Remember, the measure of success here is that everyone—*from the top to the bottom of an organization*—can answer these questions and sound like their bosses and peers.

**DON'T SETTLE
FOR UNCLEAR STRATEGIES**

Use the following Big Picture Questions to test that your strategy has been heard by asking everyone to demonstrate that they "get" the big picture. Knowing the big picture is essential to an employee's ability to prioritize and exercise good judgment. The measure of success here is that everyone—from top to bottom of an organization—can answer these questions and sound like their bosses and peers.

1. In order of priority, who are the (internal and/or external) customers or customer segments we serve?

2. What are the products or services we currently provide, and which ones, if any, need to change as we implement the current strategy?

3. With whom (and in what priority) do we partner in delivering our products or services?

4. In order of priority, who are our competitors, why is each considered a threat, and what can we learn from them?

5. How do we currently measure our success, and how might that change in the future?

6. What is the relevant history that affects current strategy?

7. Which external trends or issues (such as market, economic, societal, political, or environmental factors) are important to our strategy?

8. How does our organizational structure support our strategy, and how does our team fit into it?

9. What are three things our unit is doing to support the strategy?

Start with the leaders on your team. Introduce the questions and try to answer them together. It should take only about ninety minutes to answer the nine questions. It will take much longer when there is no agreement on the answers (which usually means the team is not aligned in other ways as well).

Ideally, your company's senior leadership will agree on the answers to the Big Picture Questions and create a brief presentation on these answers. Then, lower-level leaders should customize a version of this presentation for their own teams. The managers underneath them can repeat this process, with each leader rolling down the same Big Picture Questions to their team members and making the answers more granular for each group until there is alignment from top to bottom.

Once you've validated that everyone can explain their roles in the big picture, you're ready to talk about the technical and specialized work that will need to get done to *execute* the strategy. You can use the Knowledge Silo Matrix (KSM) tool introduced in the previous chapter to compare what capacity the team *has* in terms of technical talent to what it's going to *need*.

The data contained in the Knowledge Silo Matrix is especially relevant when it is used to assess the risk that a corporate strategic initiative is headed for failure. And the data's value is readily apparent when it drives meaningful conversations between the board and the C-suite, and then all the way down to frontline leaders.

This is the second revolutionary idea in this book. First, I gave you a quick and practical process to gather the data needed to assess your talent risk. Now, I'm going to model for you and your teams how to use the data to tackle the real-world business problems you face every day.

I want to show you how conversations change radically once you have the framework, data, and lexicon in place. We will look at the conversations from different perspectives: the board and executives (top-down), the middle and frontline managers (middle), and the frontline experts (bottom-up). By the way, technical experts can be found at all levels of the organization, and leaders at all levels are sometimes not technical at all. That is part of the challenge.

STARTING AT THE TOP—THE BOARD'S ROLE IN MANAGING TALENT RISK

The co-chair of NACD's blue-ribbon committee report on the board's role in talent development spoke to me about the role corporate boards play in giving top management feedback and guidance on talent risk.[23] "Boards have a critical role to play in CEO succession and strategy. When boards talk about strategy, they should also consider talent risk," she said. "Smart companies know if you don't have the right team, you can't deliver on your strategy. While the board must leave day-to-day operations to management, it is their role to ensure that management is thinking deeply about talent and committing sufficient time and resources to the focus."

The NACD report concluded with "Ten Imperatives for Effective Oversight of Talent Development Programs." Here are the top four:

1. To meet future challenges, successful organizations establish multiyear, multilevel internal pipelines of talent. It is vital that the board recognizes that talent, strategy, and risk are inexorably linked.

2. Oversight of the company's talent development efforts should be a full board responsibility, with the actual planning and execution owned by management. The standing board committees can oversee the talent development associated with their respective areas of oversight.

3. The full board should view human capital through the lens of strategy and risk, with committees providing input to the board on talent development in their respective areas as appropriate. In addition to reviewing the talent factor related to every strategic initiative, the board agenda should allocate time—at least annually—to take a deep dive into human capital development.

4. Directors should request that management provide a talent component in every strategic initiative presented to the board. Just as an institution is built on the flow of talent upward and across the organization, oversight can be viewed as cascading

23 "BRC Talent Development: A Boardroom Imperative," The National Association of Corporate Directors, 2013.

downward. The talent discussion must be ongoing and supported by a variety of metrics.

These imperatives provide excellent guidance for corporate board directors but do not go far enough in explaining how to do this work. Directors who sit on talent committees can use this chapter to guide CEOs and CHROs on going beyond traditional succession planning to ensure every strategic initiative has a robust talent plan to back it up.

MODELING TRM CONVERSATIONS FOR EXECUTIVES

Browse this list of familiar questions that executives ask, and consider for yourself just how well the executives are informed about risk once they get the answer.

- How many Full-Time Employees (FTEs) and Contractors do we have? What's the ratio?

- How many Level 4 Engineers are available for this project?

- How is our diversity profile shaping up?

- How old is everyone and when are they going to retire?

- Do we have enough people to throw at this problem?

- We need "Chris" on this work. What is it going to take to free up Chris to help us out?

- How's the team doing? I know they're under a lot of pressure. Are they holding it together?

- I just spent a fortune on training. How come no one appears to know what they're doing?

Executives cannot make critical business decisions based on the answers to these types of questions.

The table below shows examples of these current, poor questions that form the basis of most TRM conversations compared to new, better questions that executives *could* be asking.

Notice that in every new question in this table the conversation steers toward a data-driven discussion that is quick and clear. Also, notice that the questions can be asked and answered by stakeholders at all levels of authority in the organization. Finally, notice that the questions drive collaboration in answering the questions logically. You and your teams can sit on the same side of the table to answer these questions rather than across the table from each other in negotiation or confrontation.

Current Questions	New Conversations
Can I have more head count?	Can we look at my team's risk profile on my KSM and see if it is acceptable or whether we should be adding or reallocating head count?
Do you have enough Level 4 Developers?	Which silos on my KSM have sufficient coverage with our current experts, and where do we have potential gaps or bottlenecks?
How many Full-Time Employees (FTEs) vs. Contractors do we have? What's the ratio?	Does our expertise lie within our employee base or within our contract resources? Are we OK with the risks associated with that mix?
What is the average age or tenure in our department?	Regardless of age, what critical expertise is held in the heads and hands of each employee?
How will we survive if our expert retires?	What is the plan for transferring our retiring expert's critical knowledge in silos A, B, & C to replacements before he or she departs? How will this effort be prioritized relative to other work?
Do we have enough staff for our new initiative?	Let's run some scenarios using the KSM to assess the risk of reassigning staff from legacy roles to new roles.

(Continued . . .)

Current Questions	New Conversations
How can we free up our best legacy people to invent our next big thing?	Which silos on the KSM rely on the experts we want to free up, and who is available to take on those legacy roles?
What will be the effect of this downsizing?	Let's run some scenarios using the KSM to assess the risk of losing specific staff in a downsizing.
How do we engage our high-potential employees in the future of the company?	Let's show all of our employees how they can see the wide variety of technical silos available for them to learn and help us grow our company.
I may have some under-utilized resources in my team. How do I deal with that?	Let's look at the KSM and use it to level the workload and ensure everyone is well deployed.
I want to share work between regions or around the world. How do I know that they can handle it?	Let's ensure that resources sharing the same Knowledge Silos are sufficiently consistent with a common expert (marked purple) on the Knowledge Silo matrix.
I just inherited a team. How do I figure out what they do?	Let's see the new team's Knowledge Silo Matrix and ask the Big Picture Questions to learn about the team in detail.
My team just got reorganized over the weekend. Now what?	Which silos did I pick up in the reorg and which silos did I give up? Which people did I pick up in the reorg and which people did I give up? What has changed about the answers to my Big Picture Questions?
We're rolling out a new system and have been through 40 hours of training, and nobody seems to know what to do. Now what?	Let's clarify which silos each person needs to learn and use the Skill Development Plans to ensure each person knows their "to-do" tasks and can pass the test to ensure they are ready.
I'm thinking of moving important work to a new location. What might happen to my most critical talent?	Let's run some scenarios using the KSM to assess the risks associated with the move.

Current Questions	New Conversations
We need to stand up a new facility. What's it going to take to get it staffed?	Let's run some scenarios using the KSM to assess who can be freed up to help build the new organization and decide what the new organization should look like. For instance, which silos will need to be functioning in the new location and by when?
We have a team of 3 experienced employees and have added 24 new hires to "help" ship our product in a tight timeline. Now what?	As each new hire comes on board, in which silos will they appear as yellow? How do they fit in the Big Picture? Let's customize a Skill Development Plan to target their onboarding to ensure quick and efficient contributions and limited problems.
[Prior to a merger] We're blending 2 teams after a merge. What are we going to do with the new people we are about to inherit?	Who was purple on the Knowledge Silo Matrices before the acquisition and who will be purple going forward?
[After a merger] Are they Old Company or New Company?	In which silos do they work now? What do they do for us now?

Executive–Outsourcing Conversations

Sometimes the stakeholders in the conversation are outsource partners. Over the last twenty-plus years, staffing technical organizations has taken on many forms, from all full-time employees to fully outsourced models and many variations in between. In the early days of the outsource revolution, I watched senior managers say, "Don't worry about that, we'll *just outsource it*," implying that the problem would be solved by the mythical outsource partner who would magically know what to do once we hired them and gave them the keys. Money would be saved, deadlines would be met, and problems would evaporate. In reality, the results have been mixed, and executives all over the world have had to rethink their position on the value and risks of outsourcing.

Here's how outsource talent risk can be discussed using this new model:

> "I think we can all agree that a percentage of our work-force should be outsourced. I'd like to know which silos will be kept in-house and which ones will be staffed by outsource partners. I'd like to know whether the expert (marked purple) who sets the standard for that silo is outsourced or in-house.
>
> "Once we know which silos and purples are going to be outsourced, we can analyze the risks we're facing. Then, at minimum, I'd like to know that there is a Skill Development Plan for each outsourced silo that will be used as a 'requirements document' to clarify our expectations for tasks, service levels, and quality. We should also make sure our outsource partners can paraphrase the answers to our Big Picture Questions. We cannot expect a successful outsourcing of this silo if we're not clear on what we want."

Let's face it, most companies that outsource a portion of their work are disappointed in their outsource partners. One executive I met recently was so deeply disappointed that the only solution he could see was to fire the outsource partner and hire another firm. I think the real trouble might be that his team isn't doing their part to clarify expectations. They know what they hate—turnover, missed deadlines, quality problems, etc.—but can't say for sure what they want. The conversation above would help them clarify expectations tremendously. With that backdrop, here's how the outsource partner could respond:

> "Thank you for providing the Big Picture Questions and the Knowledge Silo Matrix as context so we can better understand our role in your business. Our contract will include providing experts who will *set and maintain* the

standard for silos A, B, D, and F. We'll prepare a Skill Development Plan for each silo so the standard is clear, and you can provide us feedback as needed. We'll also provide a minimum of three full-time resources who can execute consistently on the standards for those four silos.

"For silos C, E, and G, we'll provide a minimum of five full-time resources who *consistently follow the standard set by your expert.* When we introduce a new resource to serve your team, we'll prepare them for work by using the Skill Development Plan for each of their silos, and we'll prove they are ready for work by having them answer any test questions your experts would like to ask.

"Monthly, we can review our shared KSM and have a brief conversation about the talent risks faced by any changes to our staffing so we can work together to mitigate risk and reduce surprises."

This conversation can help everyone who relies on outsource partnerships to be aligned regardless of whether they are client or vendor, executive or frontline.

WINNING THE MIDDLE—MIDDLE AND FRONTLINE MANAGERS

Middle managers will benefit from clearer expectations, especially during the churn of reorgs and the challenges of unclear roles. Here are some more examples for them.

Frontline Manager—Reorganization Response

During my first two years as a manager at Microsoft I went through four reorganizations and had five different directors. I got so good at moving that I could pack my entire office in less than an hour. I often found out about the change by seeing the moving boxes leaning against my desk on a Monday morning. That much change can be disruptive, and I learned quickly that my role as a manager was to get my team back to work and productive as soon as possible.

Reorganization does not have to be painful if you have a clear way to get aligned on the future state. Here's how an engineering manager for Costco IT tackled the news of changes in her organization using our process.

> "I just read the email announcing the reorg and explaining the basics of our new reporting structure. I understand that you're my new boss. After a reorganization, I know my team needs to be able to answer three questions ASAP. 1) How do I fit in the new big picture? 2) What are my new tasks? 3) How will I know I'm doing them the right way in the new org?
>
> "To that end, I'd like to show you my current Big Picture Questions and my Knowledge Silo Matrix. I'll use them to communicate what my team has been doing up to this point (Pointing at the KSM). These are our silos of knowledge and expertise and how we've deployed our team to date. Going forward I'd like to know which silos I will keep so I can prepare to hand off any silos that will be picked up by another leader. I'd also like to know which people from my matrix I'll continue to manage and which people I will pick up as part of the reorg. You can also tell me anything you know about our new remit. Once I have those basics, I can update my Big Picture and my KSM and answer the three questions above for my team so they can get back to work. Any risks we face will be clear by then, and I'll share my plan for mitigating them with you."

As you can see, this conversation is not academic or hypothetical. There isn't any angst and it doesn't take long. The outcome may not be immediately clear and complete because some of the information may not yet be available, but the framework is there to be filled out. This leader can help her team settle in to the "new normal" quickly, and that is great for everyone.

A side note that made this conversation particularly fun for me was that we didn't specifically train her to use the KSM and Big Picture this way. She did it on her own because the data was already in hand and it just made sense.

Frontline Manager–Blurred Lines and Unclear Roles Discussion

If you are a frontline manager, you almost certainly struggle with role clarity of some kind. Your peers, partners, and collaborators are not just down the hall—they are around the world. It can often be hard to know who is doing what and who is setting the standard. The talent risks include people quitting out of frustration; the cost of a mistake in missed deadlines and extensive rework can be devastating. Here's how frontline managers can get aligned on talent risk by talking with a peer manager:

> "I'd like to show you my team's Big Picture Questions and Knowledge Silo Matrix to help you understand our roles and priorities. Once I talk mine through, I'd like to get the same information from you. My goal is to ensure we're aligned so that our teams can work together well. If we uncover any disconnects, we can bring them up a level in our leadership chain and ask for some help.
>
> [Pointing at her KSM] "These are my silos, my experts (marked purple), and my priorities. Here are the purples on your team that we rely on to set the standard for us

where we share a silo. These are the purples on my team that we believe set the standard for you when we share a silo.

"As I look at your KSM, these are the silos where there seems to be some confusion. Since the silo is on your KSM, it appears your team does some work in these silos. I don't think that is their role anymore. Let's use the Skill Development Plan to figure out our overlap and get it cleared up."

This conversation allows these two peer managers to zoom in on the issues as needed. They can stay at the silo level if there is no overlap. If they uncover overlap, they can go down to the "who is purple and setting the standard" level. If there is further confusion, they can go to the task list in the Skill Development Plan to clarify roles, and if needed, they could even use the Test Questions to zoom in all the way to the keystroke level. *There is no need to operate on assumptions.* They can get in and figure out roles, tasks, and standards as carefully as the situation warrants. And if they can't figure it out on their own, they have a clear and simple way to escalate and get help from their leadership.

WORKING ON THE FRONT LINE– CONVERSATIONS FOR FRONTLINE EMPLOYEES

So far, I've shown how executives, middle, and frontline managers can do their parts, but one of the best features of mitigating talent risk using knowledge transfer is the ability of anyone at any level to self-drive the process. This is important because, even if you're on the front lines and good TRM is not being driven from the top down, you don't have to wait helplessly on the sidelines. The tools to analyze talent risk and then use knowledge transfer to mitigate it can be used at any level of the organization. Those tools can help you define your job and manage expectations every day.

If you are a frontline worker, what are some of the talent risk questions you want to be able to answer? Here are some common ones:

- What's my career path here?

- Who can I get to mentor me?

- I'm overworked and stressed, boss. How are you going to help lighten my load?

- I'm leaving. What do you want me to hand over to whom before I go?

- The new hire keeps asking for my help. What do you want me to tell her?

- I keep butting heads with my counterpart in another country. Can you call his manager?

- We have been waiting on Pat to troubleshoot that problem, so I missed my deadline. But Pat is swamped. Can you call the client and buy us some more time?

These questions are all about troubleshooting. Frontline workers don't think about this as talent risk. They think about it as a problem to solve. This is why frontline managers often spend the vast majority of their day solving problems that might have been prevented with a better plan on the front end.[24] If you are asking questions like these as a frontline employee, you're likely getting unsatisfactory answers. The problem is these questions are all reactive and shortsighted. You can't get to fire prevention (risk management) because you're too busy fighting fires.

---

24 "The Under-Management Epidemic Report 2014 . . . Ten Years Later," Rainmaker Thinking, Inc., October 2014.

Or you may not be asking these questions at all—even though you may be interested—because the questions seem too unlikely to yield useful answers. A reticence to even ask such standard questions is a problem for both frontline workers and their managers. This is because the employees that managers are most worried about—the high performers and high potentials that managers want to engage and retain—will not be satisfied with shallow answers.

This has been particularly true for Gen Y frontline employees and even more so for the Gen Z population starting to enter the workforce. Satisfying career path and talent management answers, more than any other reasons, are fundamentally why these employees are going to stay with an organization. Managers have to give frontline employees crisp answers. We're managing talent risk by getting these employees aligned with the mission of the organization and showing them how they can quickly and successfully move toward meaningful work.

The following table compares today's typical, poor TRM questions to the new, better TRM conversation you could be having as a frontline employee. Let's look more deeply into a few of the most common questions.

Current Questions	Better Conversations
What's my future here?	I can see from our team's KSM that I'm only working in 4 of our 21 Knowledge Silos. I'd like to talk over which of the other silos could be good for me to learn.
What should I write in as my personal development goals?	I'm interested in working in these X Knowledge Silos, which are business critical but currently lack capacity. Will you help me customize a Skill Development Plan in those silos?

Current Questions	Better Conversations
If I'm planning to leave the team, what should I be doing to leave my teammates in the best shape?	I'd like to begin cross-training some of my coworkers so I can be ready for the next promotion you've already mentioned as a possibility. I know that these 3 coworkers are interested in learning my areas of expertise. Can we discuss the possibility of my cross-training them and how that might happen?
I'm trying to learn everything at once. What should I be doing or learning most right now? Where should I focus my efforts?	I can see that there are 5 silos for which I'm marked yellow and supposed to be actively learning. There are about 40 skills to be learned in each silo. Let's customize a Skill Development Plan to help me focus on the timeliest skills first.
I heard one of our experts is retiring. What are we going to do?	I have already learned roughly 20 skills from each of our retiring expert's Skill Development Plans. If it would help, I can focus on the rest of the skills and going much deeper on each silo.
I have learned how to do the same new skill from 3 people and no 2 are alike in what they've said. Who do I believe?	Who is purple?
I'm not sure if I'm doing my job right. How do I know?	Which skills on my Skill Development Plan should I learn? Who is purple and can validate that I'm on the right track?

Frontline Employee—Aligning for Consistency Conversation

Let's say you sit down with your boss to discuss consistency and standards for quality work in your Knowledge Silos. You've noticed that your counterparts in another location keep sending files that approach the work slightly differently from the way your team does, and you're trying to figure out what to do about it. In the past, all you could do was complain that the rules seem to keep changing and you were sick of all the rework and missed deadlines. With your team's KSM in hand, you can now say:

> "Boss, I noticed that there are between ten and fifteen Knowledge Silos that our team shares with our counterparts in Dublin and Dubai. I've noticed that the files we share back and forth reflect subtle but real differences in how we each do the work, and this week I wasted more than five hours fixing the differences. I've tried to talk it over with them and sort it out. It seems like any one of the approaches could work. We just need to settle on one. The trouble is, no one is set up to pick the 'right' standard, so we keep going in circles.
>
> "It has become clear to me that each team having their own standard is a big reason I wasted those five hours this week. We have an expert setting the standard and marked purple in each silo for our team, but so do the teams in Dublin and Dubai. I wonder if we could bring together the three purples and get two of them to follow the third? It almost doesn't matter which one steps up, as long as the other two follow. I'd really appreciate your help sorting this out. We could bring our KSM to the managers of the other two teams and find out who they think is their purple. Then, we could use the Skill Development Plans to pinpoint the tasks where different approaches to the work are causing all of these problems. Finally, we could agree on who is 'purple for the world,' the expert setting the standard for that silo for all of us. I bet we could do this in a few hours on a Skype call. If I wasted five hours this week, I'm guessing I'm not the only one."

I think any manager in the world would be thrilled with an employee who instigated a conversation with that level of specificity, direction, and support for the mission. The manager can make a call to his counterparts who are likely experiencing some of the same frustration, and they can make a decision on what to do. Note that it doesn't require a plane trip, either. This just became a quick problem-solving call.

That is what I mean when I say the dialogue can be driven by anyone at any level.

Frontline Employee—Leaving the Team Conversation

Here's what the new, better talent risk conversation sounds like for a frontline worker who is planning to leave the team:

> "Hey, Boss. As you know, I have been invited to interview for a new role in our company next quarter. I want to begin the process of cross-training some of my coworkers so the reliance on me is reduced and we can be ready for the change, especially since I'm the expert (purple) on our team for three critical Knowledge Silos.
>
> "If we plan this right, we can make sure nobody feels like we're having a fire drill. I can cross-train people who are interested and eager to learn. And I'd like to do that over a reasonable amount of time, instead of leaving the team hanging with two weeks' notice.
>
> "Even if I don't get promoted or leave, it's not a good idea to have just one person holding unique critical knowledge. I think this is a practical move for us, regardless of the future. When I look around at the team, the people who show an interest in my silos and are in a good position to learn are these three coworkers—which could mean one backup for each silo, or one person for all three silos, or any combination of that. I know they're already busy, and we'll be very selective in what they learn so that being my backup isn't too big of a burden.

> "If you agree, I'd like to customize Skill Development Plans for them that lay out the skills and tasks needed to perform in my three silos. I'd like them to set aside a few hours a week when I can cross-train them and start to give them responsibilities in my silos. We can juggle their workload and priorities together to make that happen. In this way, I can ensure that the team has sufficient backups and your reliance on me is not overly big. Our risks will be reduced and we'll all be better poised for the future."

This is the opposite of knowledge hoarding. It's the awareness that *shared* knowledge is power.

The manager doesn't have to agree to the employee's proposal. The manager should, though, be curious about the conversation and consider things like: *Do we really need to prepare for her departure? Would cross-training be good for our team? Is this unique knowledge important enough to take action?* I'm hoping that the manager's answer is "yes" to all of those because it generally needs to be. Then, the manager can respond in a practical way:

> "I want to help work with you to problem-solve around this. As you noted, one of the problems we face is people are already too busy. We'll have to work together to prioritize KT relative to their current roles and spread it out sufficiently so we make good progress without overburdening the team."

Keep in mind the manager needs to look not only at the three Knowledge Silos that this frontline expert has brought up, but the whole picture of workload and priorities for every person. This is why we do a KSM for whole teams. We want to look at what I call the whole talent risk ecosystem so that a manager can say:

> "OK, well, if I juggle a little bit here, I take two of my yellows in lower-priority Silo 4 and free them up so they

can cross-train in those three silos with you. That will give them four hours a week to work on becoming your backup. That isn't much time. Let's review the Skill Development Plans for each of those silos to ensure we get the most critical knowledge transferred first.

"Since this change could be coming soon, they will likely be working a bit of overtime to learn some of this stuff; but that is better than pulling all-nighters if we were caught flat-footed. I also think the career path rewards and the company's commitment to their professional development will motivate them to put in the extra hours. I'll assess their interest level and get back to you."

The manager's job here is to help prioritize these changes relative to other tasks—even to the point of setting a target for time spent per week. The simple conversation that started with an employee's desire to ensure a steady footing after she leaves can save a lot of grief in the long run.

Frontline Employee—Clarifying What to Learn and from Whom

How about the frontline employee who is trying to keep pace with the changing technical environment on his team? What they commonly ask in current conversations held in business offices, in labs, and on plant floors today is: *How can I stay relevant? Who should I shadow? What should I be doing next to help the team?* Here's how the new, more focused talent conversation could go:

"Boss, I just went to the town hall that our executives ran where they laid out the vision for the next six to twelve months, and I was excited by what I heard.

"I'm doing my very best to interpret that in terms of what I can do to help. We've already discussed the Big

Picture Questions together and I'm clear on the answers. Going a bit deeper, the way I see it, in order to execute this vision that our executives laid out, some of our team's Knowledge Silos are going to become less important.

"I'm currently working in those silos and I'm going to be a good soldier and continue doing that without complaint. I know that some of us still need to spend part of our time in those silos—keeping the wheels on the bus. We have to maintain legacy systems and processes until these changes come about. But I want to make sure that that's not 100 percent of my time. While I'm helping with the past, I'd also like to prepare for our future. As I see it, we're going to need to add capacity in six or seven of our existing Knowledge Silos. They're going to become increasingly important and I want to ask: Would it be appropriate for me to cross-train in any of those areas?

"I also noticed that some of what our executives are talking about will require new silos representing new technologies and processes. As I was looking through this and analyzing it, I think there might be two or three new silos that are going to show up on our KSM pretty soon. I'm interested in learning those silos as well.

"I'd like to discuss ways that I could help define the new silos and figure out who's going to set their new standards. Again, I know I have to keep up with my current role. I'm just eager to be ready for the future."

This frontline employee is really focused on interpreting the strategy, the organization's big picture, and the implications of these changes on the team's KSM and his job role. Then, once his interpretation is validated, the employee and his manager are going to seek to add the most value possible—both in the maintenance of existing silos and in preparing for the future. That's a rich conversation.

I'm not being Pollyanna here. I know that there are many times when a frontline employee would talk to his manager like this, and the manager would shrug and say, "I don't know. I mean I look up a level above me, and I don't think anybody up there knows. We're in a tough spot, you and I." But within the confines of things the manager and the employee can control, they still have the opportunity to have the conversation.

Most important, that shrug can be the start of the alignment conversation that's needed bottom to top, top to bottom. Let's play that out as our final conversation model.

CONTINUING AN ALIGNMENT CONVERSATION THROUGH THE CHAIN OF COMMAND

If I'm a frontline employee and I ask my manager the questions about my future that I described earlier, and my manager says, "I think what you're saying is very logical. But, I mean, listen, *[shrug]* this organization is kind of old school. It keeps things close to the vest. I'm not sure I can do anything with what you're saying." Here's the new, better conversation that can happen:

> "Well, OK, boss. Our team's talent risk profile information is laid out clearly in this matrix right here. Since you agree that my questions and proposals make sense, would you be willing to take this matrix to your manager, present the data, and ask her about this? Would you be willing to try to manage up by explaining to her the possibilities we both think are logical and get some clarity around this?"

Then, the manager can go to his director, proactively saying:

> "Look, I have this Knowledge Silo Matrix for my team that shows our talent risk profile. I'm looking to cross-train

my people to increase our bench strength and maintain top productivity here, here, and here. I also want to better load-level the team so we have more capacity in these cutting-edge areas, which aligns with the strategy our top executive has set. So, I'd like to make some knowledge transfer investments in these five Knowledge Silos to reduce our talent risk and to encourage these employees, so that we can retain them. What do you think? Do these choices align with your understanding of our business strategy, acceptable levels of talent risk, and work priorities?"

You never know what might happen when two managers have this conversation. That director can now take the Matrix tool and, in a few hours or days, gather the relevant data from her other teams and then take the KSMs up a level to her vice president and say:

"I've got five of these matrices that show my teams' talent risk profile. This is what I've done between the five teams that I've got to cross-train, and to support them— to grow our best talent, to reduce reliance on unique individuals who could leave or transfer, and to make sure we've monetized all the head count you've given me. These are the new ideas I have for further reducing our talent risk and for retaining our best people. What do you think, and does this align with what you know about future strategy and goals?"

Then, that vice president can go up to the C-level and say something similar:

"For the three departments or divisions under me, each of them has thought through their talent risk profile. They're making sure that they've monetized and provided ROI for all the investments we've made in people. These are

the ideas we have for growth [or reduction, change, etc.].
I want to represent my people and talk over these options
with you in light of where this company is heading."

Finally, the president and CEO can go to the board with the same
data to inspire confidence that there is a clear talent strategy for their
company:

> "Staffing the new strategy I've proposed will require
> changes to 400 personnel in four locations spanning
> 122 different knowledge silos. Forty-three of those silos
> will be put at risk, and there are twenty-one key employ-
> ees who have been identified as at-risk as well. It will
> take us four months to update or set new standards and
> develop bench strength to mitigate these risks. If you're
> interested, I can provide details behind any of this in the
> form of a simple scorecard."

That's how the alignment conversation can flow up the chain of
command, aligning as it goes; everyone advocates for themselves and
for those below them.

Each of these new conversations on talent risk will lead to greater
alignment between peers and members of all levels of leadership. But
that alignment will last only as long as the organization is free from
change. Every new input—such as a reorganization, an acquisition,
a new system, or even a new employee joining a team—will create
opportunities for inefficiency and frustration. That is why this new
conversation needs to be embedded in your organization's culture
and owned by everyone. If you're seeking true organizational agil-
ity, you can't hope that aligning on and responding to talent risk will
happen with the language and frameworks that created the problem.
Instead, you can lean into these changes and lead with a new conversation based on data.

CHAPTER 9

Other Ways to Manage Talent Risk

FIGURING OUT THE RIGHT MIX OF EFFORTS TO KEEP AN ENGAGED, prepared, and stable workforce is a perennial issue. For instance, every time I walk into a client site I see many manifestations of how talent risk is being managed. I might start in the lobby where a candidate waits for the first of six intense interviews, thumbing through a brochure or watching a video of the company's accomplishments. Inside, in HR, he'll get a rundown on all the benefits of joining this great team. Next, I walk through the kitchen, and there is free coffee, bottled water, and soda; a manager is grabbing a cup as she heads to deliver a performance review. In the corner, a party is being thrown for birthday of the month. Across the way there's a millennial job-shadowing a boomer. In the same cube, his coworker is researching a problem on SharePoint. Down the hall in the conference room, where motivational posters cover the walls, there is a brown-bag lunch group talking over a technical topic of the day. In the boardroom, the executive team is poring over the latest high-potential reports and demographics data as they update their succession plans.

Does any of this sound familiar? There is nothing inherently wrong with most of it, yet the problem with these types of talent risk management efforts is they can be well executed and still leave big gaps and risk exposures in the talent pool you need—especially if you require highly technical people to run your company. Whatever combination of mitigation approaches you choose, you still need a plan in place to make sure any necessary knowledge is transferred.

DON'T SETTLE
FOR POOR RISK MANAGEMENT

The following are principles of any good risk management model.

1. Use a shared terminology and basic process, including shared milestones. For example, no business would let all executives operate with different financial/accounting systems. Standardize so you can be up to date and aligned.

2. Expect comprehensive/complete data throughout the whole life cycle. This means good risk management cannot be afraid to get granular—down to the keystroke if appropriate.

3. Measure and report on results routinely, relying on data and usable, easy metrics/dashboards/key indicators.

4. Predict and track the financial impact of what can go wrong to monitor ROI on the effort.

5. Integrate fully into standard business processes. Never make a decision about people without the risk data in hand, just like you'd never sign a big contract without legal counsel.

6. Keep it easy to maintain and to update.

In this chapter, we'll look at the most common ways in which senior leaders attempt to manage talent risk, and review how effective they can and cannot be.

OTHER PRACTICES THAT MANAGE TALENT RISK WELL

I've written extensively about Knowledge Transfer as a proven model for managing talent risk. In addition to KT, there are a few approaches that truly *work*.

A True Apprenticeship Program. If you've ever been around a construction site, you're likely to have seen a traditional apprenticeship in action. New recruits are sized up by being put to work on tasks that are physically challenging and often referred to as "grunt work." These tasks look pretty menial but they're actually proving grounds. How carefully does the young worker follow through on every instruction? Does he take safety seriously? Does he stay focused and get the job done without complaint? If he passes that phase, his older coworkers will begin putting him on tasks that are not critical but continue to test his skills, like building temporary structures that will be torn down before the project is finished. After a year or more, the young worker will probably have built a relationship with one of the older men and he'll be invited onto a crew where he can work alongside skilled craftsmen and begin specializing in more complex tasks until he's working independently. This process has worked for centuries. However, it can take years to train an apprentice and it doesn't scale well. For example, there is no way for a true apprenticeship to work unless the expert and the apprentice are physically together most of the time. Some companies try to emulate this approach through "job shadowing" or "rotational programs." I'll write more about them in a bit.

Certification Programs. Formal certification programs can be an excellent way to manage talent risk because when all workers receive the same training and pass the same test, there is a high likelihood of consistency. Continued education can be built into recertification to ensure that the latest techniques are known and applied by everyone. For example, PMBOK is a common standard for project managers, and if someone can show PMBOK certification, you can expect a certain level of quality and standards from their work. The downside of certification is that it is costly and time consuming to develop and deploy, but there is no doubt it is an excellent solution for high-volume, high-consistency positions like project management and quality control.

Formal Internship Programs. Internships are widely understood to be a great way for students to get experience before choosing a career path. What many people don't know is that they're really a recruiting tool for the companies who host the interns. They're a great way to reduce talent risk for several reasons. First, the company gets an opportunity to "test drive" the interns in real-world scenarios. Second, internships can increase the pool of people applying for full-time positions. If a student has a great experience as an intern, she's more likely to want to take a full-time position after she graduates. Third, it can build the company's "employment brand." If the intern has a great experience, she tells great stories about the company and invites her smart friends to join her there after graduation. All great outcomes when well executed. However, it can be a disaster when the purpose of the internship isn't understood by the managers hosting the interns. If the manager sees the intern merely as cheap labor and doesn't provide a sufficiently challenging project, the intern's fit and skill set aren't really tested. And if interns don't have a good experience, they not only won't want to come back, but they'll tell all their smart friends to stay away.

Career Mentoring Programs. To make my point here, I differentiate career mentoring programs from knowledge transfer programs because in my experience they solve two different problems. Career mentors are typically longer-tenured employees who agree to meet with one or more less-experienced and often younger colleagues to help them navigate the corporate ladder to success in the coming months or even years. Knowledge transfer is focused on the skills needed to go to work here and now. When career mentoring programs work, they work well, but there is little formal data showing that the investment in programs pays off. Typically these programs work through what I call a "dating service" model. A younger worker is matched to an older worker based on profiles, and they are invited to a kickoff lunch. They agree to meet a certain number of times to talk over the younger worker's career aspirations and make connections for the future. They aren't discussing current and future technical knowledge or skill sets. They are talking about when and where the next career move might be. Even if knowledge transfer is baked into the mentoring program, you are going to run into roadblocks. The mentor is often busy and isn't motivated in any way beyond pure kindness to help. The younger worker doesn't have a plan to use the time well and finds the exchanges exciting but awkward. Unless they make a true personal connection, the relationship falls away after the second or third conversation. Meanwhile the younger worker often secures a mentor through more organic methods, like talking to their manager or making a friend in the department. Career mentoring relationships are a good idea—and they can reduce talent risk—but a "program" isn't likely to be a predictably worthy investment.

GOOD PRACTICES IF PAIRED WITH A MEASURABLE PLAN

Formal Training. There is a time and place for classroom training, online learning, tutorials, and other forms of formal educational programs. For the purposes of this book, and with apologies to my colleagues in learning and development, I'm going to lump these methods together to make my point.

I think we can all agree that to reduce talent risk as effectively as possible, we need to ensure that the students who attend these learning sessions are measured on their ability to use their new skills when they get back to work. In my experience, this can best be accomplished by making a list of the specific tasks that each student will learn during the educational program and then giving them a specific way to measure whether they've learned. This puts them in the driver's seat when it comes to getting value out of the time and money invested in their education. They are no longer victims who have been forced to attend training. If the formal training can't clearly state and measure what the learners will be able to do as a result, then it is probably going to be a waste of time anyway.

Formal training also struggles with being timely. More than 70 percent of learning happens on the job regardless of the quality of available training. So, by definition, formal training must be partnered with structured on-the-job training to provide a well-rounded and practical solution. In this way, formal training can be an excellent supplement to a knowledge transfer program. Use formal training to hit the high-volume, predictable skills that everyone needs, and use knowledge transfer to do the rest.

9-Box Models. 9-box is commonly used in succession planning to facilitate a discussion around who belongs in a pool of potential future leaders. The idea is to identify who are the "future stars" and who is merely a "solid professional." The trouble with 9-Box is that once you have everyone on the grid, then what do you do? You can (and probably should) invest more in the "high potentials," but what happens when too many people migrate up to the top right? Or too few? Maybe the subjective nature of what is considered a "Star" ends up being too political to be of real value in ensuring you have proper successors sorted out. When someone was a star last year but not this year, what does it take to walk that message back? When the process isn't perfectly facilitated, maybe the time, anxiety, and frustration are too much of a distraction to be worth it. Instead, consider the *knowledge* that is required to be a consistent star, and grow employees with a measurable plan to get them capable of doing the work.

Succession Planning. Succession plans are an important practice for any organization and can be effective if they are supplemented with a measurable plan to grow the potential successors into their future roles. One common shortcoming of succession plans is that they typically focus only on upper management. What about succession plans for your most technical workers? What if they get promoted, poached, or transferred? Take a close look at whether some of your most unique employees can be replaced with only one successor. Often highly valued people are a rare combination of abilities that can't really be found in just one successor. Instead, we strongly recommend a succession plan *for each silo of knowledge* rather than a succession plan for *a person or a role*. The real need is not simply for a succession plan for a leader or technical expert. It is knowing what specific *work* the leader does that needs to be replaced on the team if he or she isn't able to do it. By focusing on their skills and knowledge, you can also address bench strength issues to guard against single points of failure.

High-Potential Lists. Like succession plans, high-potential lists are often populated after 9-box exercises. Again, there is nothing inherently wrong with knowing your high potentials and investing in their growth. The trouble comes when you think of this as a talent risk reduction method that is only measured by things like the total number of high-potentials on the list, how many of them get promoted, how much money is spent, how many events are run, and how many you retain in the course of a year. Instead, why not focus on the silos of knowledge where these talented individuals have potential and ensure that each of them is growing in their expertise? This will have the double value of encouraging a clear, self-directed growth path that helps them to be more satisfied in their current role, while actively preparing them to do the job you hope they'll grow into. In the absence of a detailed growth plan, being on the high-potential list can be shallow and dissatisfying.

Rotational Programs and Structured Job Shadowing. Rotational programs and structured job shadowing can be valuable techniques or a giant waste of time. The key to success is that no one should be asked to participate in job shadowing or a rotational program without a clear plan for what should be taught and/or learned. Too often the participants in these programs *don't know* what they *don't know*. So, they spend the first days, weeks, or even months figuring out what they don't know, and by the time they do, the rotation or job shadowing opportunity is over. The other problem they have is that they don't know from whom they should learn. There might be seven people on the team, and without some sort of guidance, the participants can end up learning from the person who is closest to them or nicest to them versus the most qualified expert. Instead, tell everyone involved in a job rotation or job shadow *exactly* what they don't know by writing a Skill Development Plan, and point them to the best person from whom to learn (who's purple?). Then tell them how to measure what they've learned from that person.

Travel for Training Purposes. Countless times over the years I have sat with a leader who says, "I have my best guy out for a month training our team in India [or Indiana, or wherever]. It is the only way . . ." We hate to see companies put a person on a plane to "go sort things out" or to "follow this person around and soak up what they know." That's wasteful, expensive, time consuming, and frustrating for both the expert and the learner. It can sometimes even be counterproductive when the "best guy" isn't available and they have to send "the guy who's willing to go"—regardless of actual qualifications.

Instead, we insist that employees *"never get on a plane without a plan."* We have them write a Skill Development Plan that outlines every task that will be taught by the expert who is traveling. Once that plan exists, we insist that all of those tasks are taught over the phone or through a web-meeting platform. We then measure what has been learned and only travel to cover content that wasn't learned through this approach. That way, when they do get on a plane, they are super targeted about what needs to be covered. Often the trip can be cancelled or shortened by weeks or even months. This is a much more efficient approach. It requires less time to do all the legwork to write this plan than it does to get on a plane and fly to India from North America. That is a sound investment.

Onboarding and Orientation Programs. There are certainly real benefits to onboarding and orientation programs, but most stop short of preparing a worker to actually go to work. They often introduce the company (via video or a speech by a leader) and then provide pointers to websites and other resources that may be generally useful, offer some tchotchkes with the corporate logo on them, and finally deposit the new worker with their new managers. In other words, they get you to your desk—but what happens then is up to the manager and the new hire. The outcomes are hit and miss. If every onboarding program was coupled with a measurable plan to develop the skills required to do the new job, we could reduce the time it takes workers to get up to speed by half—shaving months or even years off the time required to become productive and independent.

COMMON PRACTICES THAT DON'T EFFECTIVELY MANAGE TALENT RISK

There are a lot of practices out there masquerading as TRM. Many of these were originally conceived to serve a different talent-related purpose and have taken on a life of their own, becoming misconstrued as talent risk management practices. Some are simply bad practices and a waste of time. Let's look at a number of the most common ones, review their limitations, and debunk some costly misconceptions.

Competency Models. Competency models driven by HR can be a good tool for hiring workers with the right general abilities and culture fit, but don't put your faith in them as an active talent risk management tool. This is particularly true when it comes to any technical role. It is easy to prove my point by handing a competency model to any frontline leader or manager and asking them what they would *do* with it. Ask them to explain how it will guide their behavior and watch them squirm. It isn't hard to see why. A short list of the "vital few" competencies like "innovative thinker" or "drives for results" does nothing to lift the technical fog and provide practical guidance from the front line all the way up to the C-suite.

Instead, the act of creating and updating competencies can be a giant waste of time and a distraction from solving the real problem. Up until the introduction of the Knowledge Silo Matrix, there was no practical way to look at the unique technical "competencies" required to run a given business, so leadership was forced to settle for the vague comfort of having "something rather than nothing." Meanwhile, the frontline technical managers and workers can only roll their eyes at the vague language that is supposed to clarify their path to success. Don't be fooled into thinking that is the best you can do. If you're reading this and want to defend your competency model, I won't argue with you. Just don't settle for it anymore. You don't have to kill your competency model, but the Knowledge Silo Matrix is the natural evolution of an idea that fell short—and it is time to take that next step.

Demographic Data. While it is good to have information like the average age, tenure, and education level of your workforce, it would be a mistake to think that having this information means you're managing talent risk. Just ask yourself if reducing the average age of your workforce would make you more likely to meet your business goals, and you'll see the problem. What you really care about is the unique and critical knowledge possessed by workers of any demographic profile.

Also included in this list of "nice to have" tools that don't really help with talent risk management are:

- **Head Count and Org Charts.** Does knowing who reports to whom ensure you have sufficient capacity?

- **Job Ladders/Career Ladders.** If you know how many "Level 4 Engineers" you have, does that tell you if you have the right knowledge to maintain the unique tool, application, process, or program?

- **Job Descriptions.** Role clarity can be enhanced by a job description, but the highest priority talent risks should be mitigated at the silo and even task level. Job descriptions stop short of that.

- **Culture Statements and Mission, Vision, and Values Statements.** There can be real value in choosing language to help explain some of the softer sides of a business environment; but even if everyone memorized this information, the direct impact on talent risk would still be limited.

As you review this list, there may be a tendency to argue with my logic and point to pockets of success in your organization's current efforts. I can identify with this because in the early nineties I cofounded and ran one of the original learning and development organizations at Microsoft. My team provided training for everyone who shipped software globally. I was proud of the events we produced and the rave reviews we received from participants and management alike.

What I've learned since then is that while we did great work and we had happy internal customers, we were not methodically reducing the unseen risks that could have been readily handled if only we'd had a way to find them before they caused problems. We didn't have a way to zoom in and ensure we were solving the right problems.

Now that there is another way, we can reevaluate the investments in these other approaches to managing talent risk and ensure each of them either hits their target or is phased out as appropriate.

CHAPTER 10

What Works, Plus the Most Common Ways to Get It Wrong

ONCE YOU TAKE A CLOSER LOOK AT HOW YOU'RE CURRENTLY MANAGING talent risk, you'll be able to compare what you currently have to what you actually need. In this chapter, I'll give you a list of the attributes of all great technical talent risk management programs, counterbalanced by the ways in which we've seen clients get it wrong. A quality talent risk management effort should fall within the range provided between the good and the bad presented in each section head.

Stay simple but don't settle for shallow.

You'll know your talent risk management framework is simple enough if you can explain it to a typical executive and/or frontline worker in a matter of minutes. It should also be straightforward to maintain and so easy to use during regular business cycles that no one would consider making a decision about talent without the data in hand. The vocabulary, framework, and data should make it easy to have quick and clear conversations about talent risk.

Don't let "shallow" be a substitute for simple. If you hear phrases like "we have a good, broad-brush overview of talent," you are settling for shallow. If you think that zooming in on the detailed skills of your most critical technical experts simply can't be done, you're settling for shallow. If you think your organization's global footprint and/or deep reliance on outsourcing/subcontracting is an excuse for why your people are too complicated to analyze carefully, you're settling for shallow. C-level executives should be able to point to any individual in their organization and ask, "What does she do, and if I wanted to replace her or have more people like her, exactly how quickly can that happen?" If they can't, you've settled for shallow.

Staying simple may also require saying "no" or saying "stop." A good talent risk program is pruned regularly. For example, if you've had a competency model for years and everyone groans when it is time to update it because they do not value the data, perhaps it is no longer a best practice and it is time to stop it. In other words, avoid retaining legacy HR systems with your new talent risk management system just because they're familiar.

Get exec sponsorship but don't make managing talent risk the work of one leader.

Solid executive sponsorship is certainly the number one reason a talent risk program will be successfully launched and maintained over time. Executive sponsors have to agree on the value to be had for the effort, prioritize it relative to all of the other ways their people could spend their time, convince their leaders to participate, allocate budget to pay for it, and show up along the way to provide guidance and review the results. This is true for any effort to set and maintain a standard.

Don't rely on only one leader's sponsorship too long because leadership changes are inevitable, and loss of sponsorship can kill a nascent talent risk management effort. Corporate boards increasingly understand this and are asking for a broad-based solution. Instead of relying on one sponsor, quickly look for ways to bake your talent risk management methodology into other familiar routines.

For example, one way that organizations solve talent problems is to add head count. Executives should never approve head count without first analyzing whether existing employees are fully utilized and without knowing the plan for onboarding the new resource quickly. Before announcing a reorganization, leaders should be required to explain the impact of the reorg on their talent risk and explain their plans to mitigate the risk within the first ten days of the reorg, including metrics and deadlines. During strategy-setting and business-planning exercises, every leader should be able to explain their technical staffing requirements at the "silo" level, not just in terms of numbers. Performance reviews for all leaders should include measuring them on how well they are managing their technical talent risk.

Build a high-level exec dashboard, but make sure execs can also zoom in where they have critical risks.

Tracking a talent risk management dashboard is one of the great promises of this work. Executives expect quality data to guide decision making in every other aspect of business, and they want to be able to present this information to their boards as evidence that they have a comprehensive talent plan along with their other high-level thinking. There should be no shortcuts when it comes to managing talent risk. At a minimum, every manager should be able to discuss and easily produce a dashboard with these data points:

- Simple answers to the Big Picture questions

- Total number of silos required to execute the strategy (and percentage at risk)

- Total number of people (employees and contractors) working on a team (and percentage at risk)

- Percentage of high-risk people and silos that have plans to mitigate their risks

- Projected duration until 100 percent acceptable risk is reached

- All recent risk mitigation results (KSM color changes)

- Silos of knowledge associated with high-profile executives and succession plans for each silo (rather than simply succession plans by person)

- X number of new hires, versus Y number with customized SDP plans as part of a comprehensive onboarding plan

- A list of highest-risk, highest-priority knowledge silos in each division or business line to check against business strategy

What goes wrong is a failure of executives to routinely drill in on the data (past the dashboard level) to ensure they're aligned with the leaders in their organizations in terms of acceptable levels of risk. No one should mistake this for micromanagement. See it as a rare opportunity to ensure that the Big Picture is clear and that every tradeoff has been made to ensure focus on the best use of everyone's time.

For example, it is appropriate and advisable for executives to attend a KSM alignment meeting where they can hear five leaders representing one hundred employees present their talent risks and mitigation priorities in one hour. If any anomalies or disconnects pop up, they can be addressed real-time or through subsequent meetings. It is an incredibly efficient way for executives to support the people part of their business while keeping an eye on the successful execution of their business plans.

Design for your unique culture, but don't use your uniqueness as an excuse to get sloppy.

Nearly 100 percent of our clients will say at some point that they're "not like everyone else," and thus they need a customized version of our methodology to suit their unique culture and business environment. They say this because it is true. They *are* all unique, and it would be unwise to try to implement a program that isn't appropriate for their needs.

The trouble comes when they use the idea of being unique as an excuse to avoid managing their talent risk with a sufficient degree of discipline. The truth is that organizations are the same as everyone else in more ways than they are different. This is true because reliance on technical professionals is at the heart of managing talent risk, and over the last twenty years we've seen how predictable technical professionals can be, regardless of where they work. So let's get the basics right regardless of your culture and reap those rewards right away. Even if your top folks are "really too busy" (100 percent say this), won't "put up with any bureaucracy," or are "sick of the flavor-of-the-month solutions," they still need to level the workloads of key experts, have a succession plan for workers with unique technical knowledge, get new folks up to speed quickly, and get people back to work after big changes like reorgs or new system rollouts. If the solution solves these very real problems, it can be effective in any type of organization.

Write talent risk management strategy and plans but don't let them live separately from other strategy documents.

Most executive teams have a process for setting the various strategies needed to run their business. A strategy for managing talent risk should also be on this list of long-range thinking and direction setting, because every organization should be as clear about this issue as they are about the others. This issue is so important that the National Association of Corporate Directors suggests that every corporate board should "request that management provide a talent component in every strategic initiative presented to the board" as one of their top ten imperatives.

To this point, I recommend that every business strategy include a talent component right in the document. Executives should be able to clearly state how they're going to have sufficient *technical* talent three to thirty-six months out to execute their strategy, or the board should not accept the strategy as complete. Attempts at this are made by including head count requirements or discussing offshore or outsourced options, but while these perfunctory ideas might address talent budgets or hiring timelines, they do not sufficiently address talent risk. Take the time to include steps toward meeting the technical requirements of every business strategy to ensure more predictable outcomes.

> **Set business strategy and talent risk management strategy at the exec level, but don't forget to explain it to the front line and then measure whether they actually heard you.**

No executive team wants to live in the proverbial "ivory tower" where their vision for the future makes sense to them but the message isn't clear to their people. So they do all sorts of things to keep this from happening. They write white papers, produce PowerPoint decks, lead all-hands meetings, conduct leader training, and offer to answer questions with an "open-door" policy.

The trouble is that what is obvious to the executive team can be hard to turn into practice when you're a leader on the front line or a technical worker trying to prioritize your day. That is why any communication of strategy should include a way to measure whether it has been heard and understood. The Big Picture questions in chapter 8 of this book are a good measure of whether leaders and technical workers at all levels are clear about the business and talent risk strategies. Everyone should be able to answer them and sound like their manager and their peers to ensure there is no confusion.

Plan for metrics and then don't forget to measure.

At the outset of any project there is always plenty of talk about measurement. Operations wants to measure impact on throughput, Quality wants to measure impact on the product, Finance wants to talk about ROI, HR wants to measure engagement, etc. Everyone agrees that you get what you measure, and we all congratulate ourselves on our capacity for "measurable results."

The trouble starts when the *work* of measurement butts up against all the other ways that people can spend their time. It turns out that talking about measuring results is much easier than doing the measuring. There are a couple of tricks to ensure that measurement happens. First, make sure that those doing the measuring have a selfish motivation for keeping up the data. Frontline technical workers will measure their reduced talent risk if it helps them "graduate" a coworker who can then share some of their workload. Frontline leaders will measure talent risk if it helps them lead their teams or prepare for a big project with less stress. Directors will measure talent risk if it is required to get their projects funded. Executives will measure talent risk if their boards won't approve a strategy without it. Everyone benefits in some way from measuring and mitigating talent risk, so make sure they see and realize that benefit.

The second trick is to ensure that every bit of data has an owner. Frontline employees should own reporting on their customized Skill Development Plans. Managers should own reporting on their high-risk silos. Executives should own reporting on their enterprise risks when submitting their strategic plans and presenting to their board. The final trick to ensuring regular measurement is to simply be consistent about asking for it. Executives who start their planning sessions with pointed questions about the current state of talent data will teach the leaders on their team that this information is not optional. Since the planning meeting will be shorter and more useful if it is based on good talent risk data, everyone will be eager to do it again next time.

Start off with a big, steady push and then don't lose focus.

As with any new initiative, consistently managing talent risk requires a proper strategy, rollout plan, budgets, communication, change management training, dashboards, status updates, and—most importantly—ongoing executive sponsorship. No one would argue that this is a lot of work to set up and get going, but getting started isn't usually the problem.

Building the system is usually fairly straightforward, but continuing to maintain it once built can be elusive. This is especially true if there is a change in leadership. The best way to reduce the chance of your talent risk management effort becoming another "flavor of the month" is to embed it in the decision-making process. For example, no reorganization should be approved without a quick analysis of the impact on talent risk, and managers should not get a satisfactory performance review unless they can explain their talent risk and plans to improve it. In this way, the ongoing focus is embedded in and maintained over time.

Don't leave out the outsource partners and auxiliary players.

Since "talent" is just another word for people, it seems obvious that talent risk management would include *all* the people in an organization. Some of the people live and work near headquarters. Some work from home or from a satellite location. Some are "borrowed" from a customer or from a nearby team. Some are employees, contractors, or consultants.

The trouble comes when a leader forgets to include people who are part of their talent ecosystem but "under the radar." This includes part-time and seasonal helpers like the planners who come in during the budget cycle. It includes specialists who come in to troubleshoot big problems. It includes internal customers who share responsibilities at certain times. It includes nameless contractors who answer emails sent to a group distribution list.

When we do our talent risk analysis with the Knowledge Silo Matrix, we require leaders to list out *all* the workers on their team regardless of location or employment status, and inevitably they say something like, "Oh yeah, I guess that person *does* work for me . . . " Don't worry about the IRS rules around treating contractors like employees when it comes to assessing your talent risk. How you mitigate the risk may come into play, but assessing it using a tool like the Knowledge Silo Matrix should pose no problem.

Make it a high priority but don't leave it out of the budget (utilization).

Once you understand and prioritize talent risk, it makes sense that mitigation is the next step. Since the new data is interesting to executives, they'll often ask the leaders in their organizations to make mitigation a top priority. The leaders will then look at their employees and say the same thing. This is good, right? Making talent risk mitigation a priority should be all it takes.

The trouble is that solutions to talent risk problems can't become "unfunded mandates." In other words, leaders of all levels need to recognize that if you ask a worker to transfer knowledge as a way of mitigating risk, and the knowledge transfer plan includes thirty hours of work that must be done within one month, this is going to have an impact on the productivity of that worker. It isn't unusual for workers to put in a few extra hours to help the team, but if all the knowledge transfer must be done on top of a heavy workload, with no support for reprioritizing other tasks, the chances of success are reduced or even shut down entirely.

We recommend, for example, reprioritizing four hours per week for both experts and their apprentices so they can have that time to focus on knowledge transfer and talent risk mitigation. If the number of hours dedicated to solving the problem is agreed upon and tracked, the results are predictable.

Plan to develop internal capacity,
but don't let up on outside oversight.

One hundred percent of the organizations we support are interested in developing some degree of talent risk management capacity within their own employees, and we agree wholeheartedly that this is a good idea. This is a multifaceted undertaking that includes training executives to plan with talent-risk data, monitor their risks, and "zoom in" where they see problems. It means lower-level managers are routinely onboarding and cross-training their workers to ensure predictable capacity, and frontline workers are in touch with their managers on ways they can actively learn or teach on the job. When it works, the process gets built into the culture and DNA of an organization, so oversight is minimal.

The trouble comes in the space between setting up the system and the time in which it becomes "normal" to lead and work within these systems. During that time, it is critical to have an outside audit of the process conducted regularly to ensure the process is neither watered down nor overly complicated—two of the biggest reasons for failure.

———

As I wrap up this chapter, I want you to pay attention to how you felt while reading it. If you are confident that the thinking presented here is pretty much common sense, that your organization falls near the top of the range I've presented, and that you're pretty much good to go, consider this possibility before you move on. Is it possible that instead of hearing what I'm communicating as a mandate for change, you're hearing a voice that soothes you and keeps you comfortable with the status quo rather than driving you out of your chair, taking a list like this as a catalyst for inciting a revolution? Beware of inertia. Leaders like you are needed to bring this thinking to life in your organization.

PART III

Managing Technical Talent Risk: Case Studies

THE FOLLOWING CASE STUDIES SHOW HOW CLIENTS OF MY CONSULT-ing company have recently applied the process in this book to manage talent risk. These four studies tell the stories of two major manufacturers, a global software developer, and a leading food wholesaler—all corporations that need to maintain substantial workforces of technically skilled talent. The business problems vary. One study features a company implementing an Enterprise Resource Planning (ERP) solution; another features a company divesting itself of ERP.

At The Steve Trautman Co., we don't take sides on which business strategy is right for your organization. But we draw a *big line* in the sand on which talent risk management approach gives your business strategy the best chance of succeeding. I'm featuring both these ERP-related case studies here to illustrate that our process works regardless of which side of the fence you live on. Similarly, while some case studies show an organization managing talent risk during boom times, another illustrates using our process during an industry downturn. I've chosen these examples to show that the talent risk management approach I'm advocating is flexible and adaptive, not constricted to one type of economy. Additional case studies on talent risk management and knowledge transfer can be found at www.stevetrautman.com.

Transforming IT & Embedding TRM—A Fortune 500 Food Wholesaler

ONE OF OUR CLIENTS IS A GLOBAL LEADER IN DISTRIBUTING, MARKET-ing, and selling food-related products to commercial enterprises. It is also one of my most forward-thinking clients. Today the company is pushing the envelope in IT transformation while at the same time embedding first-rate talent risk management that will help their people navigate change, now and in the future.

THE BUSINESS PROBLEM

In the early 2010s, the company had started a major business and IT systems move to a SAP-based ERP (Enterprise Resource Planning) solution. Like many companies at the time, the complex ERP implementation was a struggle. Several years later, based on their progress to date and technologies then available to them in 2016, C-level leadership made a strategic decision that was countercultural to IT trends at the time: They would return to and invest in their legacy systems.

> **CHALLENGES:**
> ....
>
> - International return to legacy systems
> - Navigate tight timelines for the transition
> - Need for better, more available talent risk data
> - Reduce talent-related bottlenecks
> - Create agile teams of super talent for next-gen projects
> - Supply development opportunities and faster ramp-up of FTEs and contractors

For the CTO and the company's leadership team, this decision was not a retreat. It was bold, cutting-edge thinking. They had previously spent over two decades pouring IP and customizations into their legacy warehouse management, order management, and other systems that are very specific to the food service industry and to their customers. They still saw huge value in that investment—more than they were getting from the ERP solution, they decided. Results with their new SAP-based solution were getting worse, not better. That said something about the efficiency and the capability of their legacy systems. New technologies, like the cloud and services architecture, meant instead of scrapping their legacy systems, the company could modernize them. The problem wasn't the old systems; it was the old technology they were based on.

The company discontinued their SAP implementation and began to modernize the existing systems. It was immediately apparent to the CTO that he had a knowledge issue on his hands. These legacy systems were proprietary to the company, and many of the experts were already of retirement age.

At the same time, the CTO wanted to create highly agile, strike force–like teams of IT super talent that could be deployed to work on special next-generation projects. The information and business technology division as a whole wanted to attract more top-rate millennial talent by providing clear growth paths and opportunities to expand their skills. Lastly, the company needed to manage through all this change while keeping the core business running.

The food wholesaler looked to their IT consulting firm, who assessed the situation and recommended the company reach out to my company for talent risk management and knowledge transfer solutions.

THE TALENT RISK CHALLENGE

The food wholesaler's new strategy included a spending cap on SAP by the start of the next fiscal year so they could hit their corporate operating income targets. Also, the transition back to legacy systems needed to minimize disruption to the food wholesaler's various operating companies and to customers. Business continuity was paramount.

Adding pressure, the company's leaders had been urging the CTO and his team to home in on their high-priority work and "go faster." This meant working more efficiently and creating greater capacity through more high-quality, knowledgeable IT workers. Knowledgeable workers familiar with the company's business and systems were not something the food wholesaler could buy from outside sources. Talent was the scarcest commodity and they knew they would have to grow new talent themselves and do it quickly.

The CTO explained to me that if he had fifteen people, for example, who really understood the inner workings of their different systems and how they fit together, his division could only go as fast as the amount of work those fifteen people could do. The fifteen people would become his pacers. He couldn't go any faster. He knew he couldn't move quicker by multiplying his people through new hires, but he could move quicker by multiplying their knowledge. The CTO brought in my consulting firm, telling me that he liked how methodical our knowledge transfer solution was and how our talent risk tools gave his team the ability to see and manage their talent risk long term.

GETTING THE RIGHT TALENT RISK DATA

The first thing the company did was start collecting relevant and detailed talent data. It began with one of its highest priority teams—about 200 people led by the VP of operations technology. The VP's team was responsible for all the development and support technology for the company's merchandising, pricing and agreement, and supply chain teams—which include warehouse and delivery.

Her team completed their KSMs during a busy time: Fiscal year-end performance reviews were due, and teams were planning for the coming year. She had anticipated some resistance. The main concern she heard from her people were some grumbles at the outset about whether they "have time for this right now." The grumbling was quickly addressed using the KSM tool—which has been optimized for simplicity and speed—and through the VP's deft leadership. Because the tool is very low-touch, it didn't take a lot of time for her team to populate it. As a side benefit, the team quickly learned that the tool was helping with their performance reviews and year-end planning as well.

Even at the project's initial stages, the data was providing insights. The VP and her managers had a good idea as to which teams were affected by talent gaps. The KSM tool helped them to definitively pinpoint both the obvious risks plus some they hadn't been aware of. It pointed out risk areas they didn't know were so high—including systems that didn't have the support that managers would have liked, single points of failure, the potential for burnout of overtaxed experts, and where workers were perhaps underutilized.

The VP mentioned how surprised every one of her leaders and

managers were—including herself—when they saw a KSM of their team for the first time. She felt that, despite what you thought you knew or your gut was telling you, it wasn't until you actually fill out a KSM that you really understand the work that the group does. Of course, you have some sense that certain employees get credit for this or they do that, but the KSM forces you into really clarifying the critical work that each person on a team does. That was her and her managers' first aha moment—really getting the view of what's going on. The second aha was gaining a true understanding of their bench strength. Who were the key players in this group? How did the group interact? Who has the knowledge? Who doesn't? Who's established? Who's learning? As a coach, she now had the ability to see her team and know exactly where the strengths and weaknesses were.

A MEETING SETS THE TALENT RISK MANAGEMENT COURSE

Early on, the company wanted to get executive alignment on how business priorities would affect talent requirements and to determine how IT was going to approach its risk. Teresa Canady, one of our master consultants, led the CTO, the VP, and nine other IT executives on the CTO's leadership team through a talent strategy alignment meeting. In the weeks before the meeting, Teresa individually interviewed each participant for about an hour. Each executive ranked around twenty guideposts that represented strategic positions. My team has developed these guideposts over the years to best enable alignment around clear priorities and a resulting strategy. The company added two guideposts of their own.

When the group came together to discuss and get aligned in the areas of discrepancy, they considered their business priorities and what IT needed to accomplish. They looked at their capabilities and what that meant for the projects planned. Then they looked at what all this would mean for their talent demands and staffing. Did they have the right people trained with the right skills? Did they have other talent risks covered, like dealing with an aging workforce or possible challenges in attracting top talent?

One example of an area where IT executives needed to get alignment was on deciding whether they were solving for an immediate talent risk problem or a long-term one. Another example was whether the company would roll out their talent risk management solution quickly or in phases. The team agreed they were solving for a long-term problem and that they'd take a balanced approach phased in over eighteen to twenty-four months that addressed the highest risk areas first.

The alignment meeting enabled the company to look at talent holistically. The CTO told me that, for the first time, they could have an informed discussion with real facts and information and data around a knowledge-risk conversation that wasn't anecdotal or built on sound bites. Now they had the content and framework for very substantive conversations about risk. They could look at the risk associated with planned changes and know what they could do about those risks.

Teresa then made specific recommendations for addressing each risk that the company had aligned on. Overall, the alignment process was quick. Start to finish—from kickoff to final alignment—took about three weeks in mid-summer 2016. One of the first things needed, everyone agreed, was to go beyond the leadership team and do a comprehensive risk assessment for all of IT using the KSMx.

THE KSMX ALIGNMENT MEETING

Although the company's IT managers had found the KSM a very helpful eye-opener for their own single ten- to twenty-five-person teams, the data came to life in a new way when viewing whole divisions or subdivisions after a KSMx Alignment Meeting. Again, the company started this effort with the VP of operations technology's high-priority organization. Thirteen of her managers—each owning a KSM for their employees and contractors representing her 200 reports—were asked to prepare a five-minute presentation of their KSM. During the alignment meeting, each manager would talk about their KSM and what they saw as talent risks and priorities for mitigation while their peers looked on and gave feedback.

Each of the thirteen managers had looked at their knowledge silos individually and assessed their risk within their scope of control. The KSMx enabled the VP to now look at risk across her entire division as one talent ecosystem. The KSMx also surfaced opportunities that weren't being leveraged. By giving the VP and her managers detailed talent data along with a common language and framework for alignment, the KSMx helped facilitate conversations on performance management, head count, backfilling gaps in their organization's knowledge and skills, and even the technical career growth opportunities that showed up.

Here are just four immediate takeaways from the KSMx Alignment Meeting for the VP's team. First, the company has a warehouse system that is used by multiple business units. Previously, IT had not discussed knowledge of that system in a comprehensive way across all those business units; they would talk about it individually for each unit. Now the VP's team was having broader conversations and asking questions like, "Is this a warehouse capability skill that we need in our talent force, and is that capability something consistent that we can use across all our entities? Or is it really specific to each business unit?"

Second, because each of her leaders had done their risk assessment individually, certain areas and individual experts looked good. But when the team came together for their alignment session and merged the information, they found a couple of contractors were on *each* person's KSM. When they saw the full picture, those vendor partner resources became a risk because they were being leveraged by so many different teams—causing a high danger of bottleneck.

The third takeaway was the ability to expose multiple and conflicting standards of expertise. For instance, the team that uses the warehouse system in Ireland thought they were the system experts setting the standard for use—"purple" on the KSMx. The Canadian team that also used that system said *they* were purple. Then another team at corporate said *they* were purple. The VP and her managers were able to have a thorough discussion on who really was the expert, or "purple," for which parts of the system. The discussion clarified roles and responsibilities across teams.

The fourth takeaway was the insight the VP got about how she could align with her VP peers and their teams. She could ask questions like, "For the gaps and talent risks in my 200-person team—like where we lack sufficient backups—are there maybe opportunities to offset some of those risks against other teams that support us?" She already leveraged some of her peers' teams, such as the VP in security and infrastructure's team. The managers had marked some of their people as the experts, or "purple" for certain knowledge silos, but they were also leveraging the infrastructure team to do a lot of that work. Essentially, her team was using the infrastructure team as service providers. So were her people the "purple" and did she actually have gaps—or did she have misaligned roles? The VP of operations technology could identify overlapping areas and start conversations with her peers to ensure no risk was falling between the cracks of the two VP teams.

HOW THE COMPANY IS EMBEDDING TALENT RISK MANAGEMENT

The CTO and his leadership team knew they had to make their talent risk management and knowledge transfer efforts live on to be worth the investment and to support IT's new systems strategy and projects.

IT leadership knew they had to consistently stay on top of their talent risk profile just like they routinely monitor other business drivers like budgets and service metrics.

The way the CTO saw it, in IT there is always a new initiative or new flavor of the month. Their talent risk management work had to tie into their other day-to-day processes. If IT already had a performance management tool, this would augment it. If IT already had a project management process, this could support it. The CTO wanted their talent risk program not to replace but to inform other existing processes. By Q4 2016, the CTO and his leadership team had come up with a number of ways to embed managing talent risk into the DNA of the organization through existing everyday processes. Some examples are—

- The company is growing expertise across its IT organization on how to complete and use knowledge silo matrices. All managers are expected to know what a KSM is, how to fill one out, and how it informs decision-making. They are expected to keep their KSM data up to date and produce their team's KSM for their supervisor at any time. Every time they have one of these talent management conversations, pulling out the tools should be "muscle memory."

- To get new head count approved, managers have to present the need in the context of their KSM. Not only does this help clarify whether there's a real case for adding head count, it also adds further incentive to keep KSMs updated. The CTO basically said that if someone comes to him with a request for a new head count, he wants to see their KSM before he approves it. He wants to see what the person who's leaving is taking with them in terms of knowledge. Is there enough strength on that bench that maybe they could use that head count elsewhere where they're not so strong? Do they really need to rehire for that? Or do they actually need to hire more than one person?

- New leaders coming in are expected to consult their teams' KSMs to better understand the team they're inheriting. What are the specific knowledge areas the team is responsible for? Who does what? What are the knowledge relationships such as experts and learners, and where is the team strong or lacking in bench strength? Is a reorg needed—and what might that look like?

- If a new project requires a new technology or ability, someone must update the corresponding KSM by adding another knowledge silo to show their team is responsible for this new capability. The owner of the KSM must fill out which employees have the skill set, who is the expert—"purple," and who is learning the skill—"yellow." If the data isn't up to date, it's not meaningful.

- During performance reviews, managers and directors are evaluated on how well their teams have transferred knowledge and reduced the organization's talent risk. Workers are evaluated on how well they've followed their date-driven Skill Development Plans and become "green" in new skills as designated.

EARLY RESULTS OF TALENT RISK MANAGEMENT EFFORTS

The company's IT division is still in the process of embedding their new talent risk management throughout all IT and mitigating risk, but some results have already been achieved.

A Smooth Transition Back to Legacy and Modernized Systems

One of the IT teams the company knew was at high risk from the outset was the support for their meat companies. Those specialty companies were moving to modernized technology and there would be team talent gaps. With the risk assessment and knowledge transfer processes so new to these IT teams, their fear was that they *wouldn't have time for this* and it *wasn't going to help.* The VP of operations technology put them through the risk assessment anyway.

The leader of that team completed the KSM, and then he and some of his team members also went through the knowledge transfer training and created Skill Development Plans. The team leader determined afterward that, rather than a waste of his time, he "should have started the process earlier because this was helping the transition to the new technology in a more structured way."

One of the VP's main concerns was that, as they go through the IT transformation and expect people to work in a different way—and not only work in a different way, but work in different technologies—they needed a tool that helped them make sure that none of her people would get lost along the way. She knew she had to bring her people along as the teams went through the transformation and she told me that my company's process has proven a powerful tool for this.

An Early Win Solving for the IT World's Problem of "Mitch"

The company had a big win early on unclogging one of its chief bottlenecks that had long hampered IT progress. When the CTO first joined the company a few years beforehand, the IT division had several important projects that were running behind. At the time, the CTO kept going to project meetings and asking questions about the delays, and the same name kept coming up. Over and over and over, he heard about "Mitch." *"Well, Mitch needs to look at this and tell us how to work, but he just has so much on his plate."* So many projects—this one guy. The CTO was beginning to realize that although he was the chief tech officer of a tens of billion-dollar corporation, he could only go as fast as "Mitch." The bottleneck.

"Bottleneck" sounds like a bad thing, but bottleneck people are the most valuable players on your team with some of your business's most critical unique knowledge. They are typically great workers—ones you'd never want to walk out the door—but they are bottlenecks because their knowledge is not shared enough. The CTO pointed out that this was the third major corporation where he has led IT and this has been a major issue in every place. He even went on to say that he would guarantee that "Mitch" is a common problem in IT shops across the country. He felt that, until he found our methodology, he had never really seen anything as clear, as concise, as scientific, or as methodical for tackling the problem of the "Mitches" of the IT world.

The company's first knowledge transfer project was to transfer "Mitch's" knowledge across many people. We implemented our three-step Knowledge Transfer Solution to share the knowledge. "Mitch" got to test everyone's progress by using our test questions until he was satisfied. The CTO reports that since then the company "can move much faster as an organization because we transferred that knowledge." And if "Mitch" decides to retire tomorrow or leave the company for any reason, IT teams can march on while meeting deadlines.

Creating Agile Teams

The company's CTO and other IT executives feel they are having real success in being able to create agile teams that have the knowledge they need to move much quicker. Of the more than 130 highly skilled experts who were working on the conversion back to a modernized legacy system in the summer of 2016, many were needed on other strategic projects as soon as possible. By mid-Q4 2016, enough workers had been freed up to move on to their next-gen work. Also, if IT does lose a critical employee now, the CTO reports that the loss isn't as debilitating as in the past.

Better Organization of Teams and Job Roles

One example of a data-driven win recently happened in the company's cloud area. A star IT manager left the food wholesaler for another opportunity. It was a regrettable yet unavoidable loss. Before departing, this manager came to the CTO with his KSM in hand saying, "I want to replace this job." The CTO and he talked through the manager's KSM. The manager said, "I want to replace this job, but I don't think we have to do it at the manager level. I think we can do it at a lower level."

As the two looked through the talent data, the CTO agreed that the manager's suggestion was probably true. Another manager was available who could take on the team's supervision while a new analyst was needed to do the technical work of the departing manager. But when the CTO considered how much work there would be in those key knowledge silos moving forward, he told the departing manager not to replace himself with another manager or a frontline analyst. "Replace yourself with *two* analysts," the CTO advised. Instead of just routinely replacing a departing manager, management was able to make a smarter talent decision based on real data and meaningful conversation.

Millennial Recruitment

The company has locations in some of North America's centers for biotechnology, healthcare, and the energy economy. When the CTO first took the helm of the IT function, people would tell him, "You do know we're competing with energy companies and big biotech, right? They can pay for all the best IT talent, so we get the second rate." But the CTO refused to believe that he had to live with that fact. He set a strategy to attract the best and brightest, especially millennials.

Today, his IT division competes on several unique selling points, starting with work environment. If you're a techie and a foodie—what a great place to come to work, notes the CTO. As a wholesaler distributing food-related products and services, the company collaborates with top restaurants and chefs all the time through their work. As a highly technical company, the wholesaler uses some of the newest technologies and agile methodologies that the slower energy companies and healthcare companies haven't yet embraced.

Today, the company can offer talented millennials the ability to move around, to be taught a variety of technologies and skills, and to quickly gain different work experiences. They are not going to be pigeonholed. Their IT division has a world-class knowledge transfer process to make these career goals a reality—something that has proven a big selling point for millennials.

New Technology Rollouts & Process Changes—a Fortune 500 Manufacturer

A FORTUNE 500 MANUFACTURER WAS IMPLEMENTING A NEW ERP (Enterprise Resource Planning) software system throughout its North American plants as part of an effort to standardize and integrate its business processes. The new Oracle software would unify the organization's various legacy systems into one accounting, purchasing, inventory, and human capital management system that provided a superior range of real-time data. The scaled, plant-by-plant implementation of this software would directly impact not only how quickly the manufacturer could begin to realize cost savings, but also, in the short term, the speed at which each plant could perform routine departmental responsibilities.

CHALLENGES:

- Expensive redundant legacy systems and roles
- Inconsistency between locations
- Too few experts
- New software learning curves
- Disruption of normal business functions during rollout

THE BUSINESS PROBLEM

The first ERP rollout had occurred at their eastern city plant using a traditional training approach. This plant took twenty-eight days to close the books after go-live. Employees had to work late nights and straight through the weekends to make it happen in those twenty-eight days. It was a chaotic mess. The Midwest plant would be the second plant to roll out the ERP solution. Their accounting team needed to close their monthly books using the new software within *seven days* of the software's go-live date at their plant. Adding to the complexity, the Midwest plant was four times larger than the first rollout plant.

One advantage the Midwest plant did have was that in the fourteen months since the eastern plant's software deployment, the ERP system had matured. One expert estimated the improvement to the software environment was significant—possibly enough to cut the previous benchmark of twenty-eight days by half. But this still left the Midwest plant team well short of their seven-day goal.

> *"Our ultimate goal was to close the books accurately in a reasonable amount of time—which in our case was seven workdays . . . We needed to limit the business interruption, make sure our results were reported accurately, and get people back to activities that add value to our bottom line. That was the challenge."*

> —Controller, Midwest plant

THE TALENT RISK CHALLENGE

The biggest talent risk roadblock? A *single* individual—the Director of ERP Special Projects—was the only person who understood the ERP system. He would be the one training the account department. One person with all the information was not only a huge potential single point of failure, but the company learned with the previous rollout that a single overworked and overextended expert shouldering so much of the training and technical support would quickly cause frequent bottlenecks.

Also, the manufacturer needed an alternative to the "one-size-fits-all" classroom-training model. This model had wasted employee time in the initial rollout because everyone was forced to listen to info not relevant to them.

> *"People were frustrated [with the traditional classroom approach]. The pace was too slow for some. The pace was too fast for others. For half the audience, the material wasn't targeted specifically for their roles. For the other half, it was spot-on, but it didn't go deep enough for what they would need to do."*
>
> —Controller, Midwest plant

The alternative training approach needed to include tools that would help non-teachers train their peers, increase knowledge retention, and enable rapid knowledge transfer in palatable doses.

The head of the IT professional development and consulting firm that was working with the manufacturer assessed the situation. He felt the talent risk was far too high for the rollout, so he contacted my team.

Whenever businesses experience technical or process changes, the goal is to get people clear on their roles and back to work as quickly as possible. We don't think organizations should settle for retraining that takes four times longer than necessary. We should not have to ask our best people to work through weekends and forgo vacations for months on end because we're still "in the midst of change." And we can't sacrifice on the altar of change the benefits that made the change attractive in the first place.

ADDRESSING THE TALENT RISK

Rather than rely on their vendor or their sole expert to "do more training" this time around, the company needed a new approach that would reduce the potential for bottlenecks. We suggested that they develop a first-tier of ERP "super users" at the Midwest plant who would take on some of the training work and answer basic questions after go-live, allowing the expert to handle more complex issues.

The manufacturer chose to do a pilot project using our talent risk management and knowledge transfer tools. The ERP expert who had led the eastern plant's training would again lead the training at the Midwest plant. But instead of being the only person in charge of training, the expert would use these tools to develop twenty non-IT super users from within the plant's accounting team, who would then mentor their remaining coworkers and deliver first-tier technical support. Managerial support would be provided by the pilot's executive sponsors: an area VP and Controller, the Controller of North American Operations, and the General Manager of HR for Corporate and Global Operations. The on-location manager—the Midwest plant's Controller—would set clear expectations, maintain urgency, remove obstacles, and hold the Midwest team accountable to its goals. Once this system was built, the manufacturer could reuse the new training model for future ERP rollouts at a dozen other plants.

A Defining Moment: Make a Complete Stop of What Doesn't Work

The ERP expert and lead trainer—who was just getting familiar with the knowledge transfer tools—had already scheduled four days of traditional classroom-style training with nearly forty Midwest plant employees. The super users, along with their apprentices, were essentially going to sit through the "one-size-fits-all" approach that had failed at the eastern plant. The timing of this classroom training also posed a knowledge-retention risk: Apprentices would not have hands-on experience with the live ERP system until four months after these long lecture sessions.

This traditional classroom training approach immediately raised a red flag. We advised that the training should be completely retargeted to developing the super users. The priority would be to replicate the knowledge of the ERP expert twenty times, so that those twenty super users could then train the rest of the Midwest staff—allowing the lead expert to pop up to a more strategic level.

The expert scrapped the classes and focused instead on his super users. He used Skill Development Plans to train them in exactly what they needed to know in a series of short one- to two-hour sessions. The super users answered designated test questions to prove that they were getting the details right. They also learned how to access documentation that would help them train their colleagues as the need arose.

To me, the ERP expert is one of the real heroes of this story. He had the courage to speak up and stop "doing it the old way." Doing the same old training in the same old ineffectual way and bolting on a few talent risk ideas or incremental changes would guarantee failure. This ERP expert's decision was a turning point in the program's overwhelming success.

Assessing Risk and Getting Alignment

After the decision to make a clean break, the ERP expert and the Midwest plant team first assessed their risk using the Knowledge Silo Matrix (KSM) so that management could map who on the accounting team needed to learn which specific ERP knowledge areas. See Color Insert 4 to see a part of their Knowledge Silo Matrix (KSM).

> *"The KSM shows you from a managerial standpoint where you're weak and the areas you need to strengthen. You see this when you really sit down and profile your workforce. So, that's a must. It has to happen everywhere we go [to roll out ERP at other plants]."*
>
> —Director of ERP Special Projects

With the KSM data, the Midwest plant's team could quickly get aligned around which ERP knowledge areas were most important to teach to whom. General Ledger and Inventory Silos were the priority, so that was the first area of focus.

Creating the Plan and Mitigating Risk with Knowledge Transfer

The team then created the detailed knowledge transfer plan to mitigate the risk. We helped the manufacturer write Skill Development Plans (SDPs) for each knowledge silo—first a master SDP per knowledge silo and then customized SDPs for individual super users and later individual apprentices. The customized plans (see Figure 5) showed which skills an employee was committed to learn, ordered in terms of priority, and a date was affixed by which the employee should have learned the skill.

> *"Once we had the customized SDPs developed, you could assign accountability to the person who needed to learn. It took the responsibility for the training away from the single person who had a lot of the knowledge and put that responsibility on the individuals who needed to learn it. I think that ultimately proved to be much more productive than the route we had been heading down."*
>
> —Controller, Midwest plant

Skill and Task	Sequence	Test Questions	Due Date	Actual Date	Resources
General Ledger Management					Mentor: A.G.
Execute the Accounting Monthly Tactical Plan	1	1,2,15,19	8/9	8/9	GENERAL LEDGER ACCOUNTING MONTHLY PLAN - GARY 2013
Troubleshoot the general ledger and DVA	2	1,2,4,5	8/9	8/9	GENERAL LEDGER, GENERAL LEDGER DVA SUB LEDGER ACCOUNTING, L-DVA_4
Pull trail balance report and cost statement	3	1,2,3,4,5	8/9	8/9	GENERAL LEDGER, GENERAL LEDGER REPORTING, L-REPORTS_DVE_3, PART 1 & 2
Write a journal entry thru approval and posting	4	1,2,3,4	8/9	8/9	GENERAL LEDGER, GENERAL LEDGER JOURNALS, L-JOURNAL ENTIRES_DVJ-2
Extract month end statistical reports	5	1,2,3,4	8/9	8/9	GENERAL LEDGER, GENERAL LEDGER STATISTICS, L_GENERAL_STATISTICS L-DVA_1
Build month end allocations via the workbench	6	1,2,3,4	8/9	8/9	GENERAL LEDGER, GENERAL LEDGER ALLOCATIONS, L-GENERAL_ALS_A1 WORKBENCH
Analyze, compare, and troubleshoot cost center range XXxx thru YYyy	7	1,2,4	8/9	8/9	GENERAL LEDGER, GENERAL LEDGER COSTING, GL_FLEXFIELS_COA_2
Read BOL	8	1,2,4,6,18	8/9	8/9	GENERAL LEDGER, GL STRUCTURE, INVENTORY KEY NATURAL ACCOUNTS - BOL DY 4

Figure 5. A partial image of a Skill Development Plan (SDP). This is a customized SDP for an apprentice of the General Ledger silo of the Midwest plant's accounting team. Some data has been changed to protect client confidentiality.

Test questions were assigned for each SDP skill to confirm that the right knowledge had been effectively transferred (see chapter 7). The test questions are one of the most important assets of three-step knowledge transfer—they give the process teeth via a metric for whether critical knowledge has transferred. Apprentices could see what was expected of them and drive their own learning. Super users and other mentors could see clear priorities for what to teach to whom and which knowledge tests to apply. And the team's manager could track skill level status to ensure accountability for results.

The Midwest Plant's Management Embodies a Best Practice

In addition to managing their risk successfully, plant managers made sure everyone up and down the chain of command could follow the pilot's progress. The controller at the plant clearly communicated to his team their knowledge transfer goals. Then he maintained a sense of urgency and personal responsibility by making the knowledge transfer a team priority throughout the three months leading up to the go-live date. He also understood that when learning is observable, valued, and credited, it reduces a team's risk of failure and builds employee engagement. He coined the term "The Greenies"—the color showing skill competency on the KSM. When an accounting team member passed her assessment for the final skill in a silo, the controller would send a lighthearted email to the entire team celebrating that the employee had become a "Greenie." The acknowledgment served not only to recognize the individual achievement, but also to highlight a short-term win for the team, bringing them one step closer to ERP self-sufficiency as a department.

CLEAR, MEASURABLE RESULTS

The initiative was a clear success. The Midwest plant accounting team met their stated goal to close the books within seven business days of their first month of ERP go-live. In successive months, the team further reduced their closing time. This was a clear improvement over the original rollout group.

ERP	MIDWEST PLANT (w/ Knowledge Transfer)	EASTERN PLANT (w/ Traditional Approach)
1st Month Live	7.5 days to close	28 days to close
2nd Month Live	7 days to close	17 days to close
3rd Month Live	5 days to close	12 days to close

Table 1. Productivity levels during and after ERP launch

In addition, employees grew measurable skill sets within the short timeframe allotted, while maintaining their regular workload. From July to September, thirty-four of the Midwest plant's accounting team each learned up to a total of 131 new skills in up to six ERP knowledge silos and passed their knowledge assessments given by the mentor. This mitigated all priority knowledge risks on the team's Knowledge Silo Matrix (KSM). Color Inserts 4 and 5 show the "before" and "after" team KSMs.

The Midwest team was soon months ahead of where the eastern team had been in rolling out the same ERP solution. The Midwest team definitely benefitted from the lessons learned by the eastern plant employees. However, operations at the Midwest plant were far more complex than the smaller eastern plant, adding a layer of complexity that the eastern plant did not face. The risk assessment, knowledge transfer, and revamped training methods clearly contributed to the Midwest team's rollout success. The less time spent on the rollout let employees at the Midwest plant move more quickly to value-adding activities.

REAL COSTS SAVED— Midwest Plant Accounting Team Employee Hours	
37 Employees and Managers	7770 estimated business hours/month
20.5 Business Days Saved **(7.5 day to close versus 28 days)**	144 hours saved per employee
Total Hours Saved in 1st Month Alone:	5310 total hours saved that could be put toward value-adding & cost-saving work

Table 2. Cost savings attributed to knowledge transfer process.

The manufacturer experienced long-term benefits such as establishing a model for faster, smoother ERP rollouts at other plants; greater team communication, collaboration, and knowledge sharing within the Midwest plant and cross-locations; and establishing tools that remain useful for hiring, onboarding, continuing staff development, and preparing future mentors.

> *"One thing that's most telling: There isn't anybody here saying, 'I don't know how to do my job.' 'I haven't been trained.' The issues we're having are more, 'How do we get better?' 'This report we thought we'd have in fifteen minutes is taking us three hours to run. How do we improve that?' . . . It's to the extent where there were a couple of people in from the eastern plant to help us out and they said that we were looking at things and asking questions that they didn't ask until they were rolled out for six months. That shows we were very, very well prepared."*

—CONTROLLER, MIDWEST PLANT

Reorganization & Downsizing— a Fortune 500 Manufacturer

REORGANIZATIONS ARE ALWAYS A CHALLENGE, AND THEY ARE EVEN more difficult during tough economic times when cost cutting is required. This case study shows how an IT director of software systems at a global manufacturer used talent risk tools to manage an unbelievably difficult situation that included laying off 60 percent of his team and relocating some of his most technical work, all while shutting down redundant systems.

CHALLENGES:

- Reorganization planning
- Cost reduction and downsizing
- Centralizing support teams
- Reducing complexity of IT systems across locations
- Planning layoffs and retaining knowledge
- Maintaining daily work with fewer people

Within a little over two years, this director has successfully reorganized and reduced costs while still meeting his productivity goals. He has also embedded talent risk management and knowledge transfer tools into the business culture, allowing him and his team to not only manage their daily work but also use their data to manage up.

THE BUSINESS PROBLEM

A Fortune 500 manufacturer had ten decentralized teams of technologists and engineers at various plants who ran the systems and software that keep its manufacturing equipment going. Each plant had its own team of software engineers. The systems at these different plants did the same basic thing. But the manufacturer had bought the plants as separate companies over the years to create their corporation, so the evolution of each system was different. The platforms were different. The programming languages were different. The business approaches were different. Thus, each plant site had its own system with its own unique team of specialists to look after it. The manufacturer decided it needed to reorganize its workforce and streamline its systems to achieve more centralized technical support for its plants.

THE TALENT RISK CHALLENGE

The company's CIO and its global plant systems director had been given a mandate to reduce operational costs. One clear way of reducing costs was to reduce the diversity of technology across its plants and create economies of scale. A handful of optimized common systems would be cheaper to maintain. At the time, the manufacturer was running more than 800 different plant systems using dozens of different software languages. Simplifying all this complexity should, in addition to producing economies of scale, have the added benefit of limiting future technological risk and talent risk. IT executives knew they wanted to streamline and centralize, but they didn't know what exactly that reorganization should look like. Would these be geographically centralized teams or virtual ones? How many teams would be needed and who would be on them? Would the new teams be centered around a system function rather than a plant, and if so, which functions from which systems? Lastly, how would they know they had the right knowledge and skills on the new teams to pull this off?

Just as the planning of the reorg was getting underway, the manufacturer's industry took an economic hit. Funds that potentially would have been available started to dry up. Any thoughts the plant systems director in charge of the reorg had about relocating individuals to geographically centralized teams evaporated. The director would need to plan a solution that took greatest advantage of where his most knowledgeable people were right now. In addition, he had to reduce head count.

He had a pressing talent risk around the ability to assess and move his workforce's technical knowledge. Before people were transferred to a new team or let go, the manufacturer first needed to make sure the company retained the critical system knowledge that each worker had been responsible for. Second, the manufacturer needed a way to quickly build up the knowledge required in others so it could then replace the current systems with a common system for that function. People who had worked for decades on, for example, support in a heavy equipment environment using FORTRAN might be moving to real-time application systems using C++. The company needed to know with justifiable confidence that none of their business-critical knowledge was walking out the door and that remaining members on new teams had been sufficiently trained before assuming new responsibilities.

This also presented a serious operational risk because, while all this change was occurring, these plant support teams would still have to perform their daily work to keep the business running.

USING THE KNOWLEDGE SILO MATRIX
TO PLAN A REORG

Looking first at operational needs and current technologies, the plant systems director and his managers, with prompting from the CIO, had decided on a strategy to create a handful of core, centralized teams from the original ten plant-based teams. Each core team, regardless of who its members were and where they sat in the world, would look after only the systems across the corporation that supported a certain function, such as quality control or scheduling. The director could then task each new team with commonizing that function to run on just one system.

> *"What I was doing was going from a federated, plant-based team structure to a centralized, function-based team structure. I wanted to regroup the organization into more sensible teams so that similar functional areas were together. Right away I was asking, 'What knowledge do I have?' and 'Where is it?'"*

> —THE MANUFACTURER'S DIRECTOR FOR
> GLOBAL PLANT SYSTEMS

My consulting team got involved by showing the director that our Knowledge Silo Matrix (KSM) would not only assess his people's relevant knowledge quickly, but was also the optimal tool for testing scenarios and planning the shape of his reorganization. He could account for talent risk factors when envisioning his reorg and establish realistic, measurable timelines for the transition.

A Reorg Based on Talent and Knowledge, Not Just Head Count and Job Titles

The plant systems director began planning his reorg using the KSM to map out the current state of his 160 people, their knowledge silos, and related talent risks. Working with his management team, the director began to see where the knowledge and skills resided to run their 800+ systems. The KSM painted a detailed and clear answer to his talent questions. Who were the experts in which systems? Who was untrained? Where was there ample bench strength? Where were there glaring knowledge gaps? With the current state as a baseline, the director could then plot different scenarios that drew his people into centralized, function-based teams and evaluate what this would do to his talent risk and the projected knowledge transfer hours needed to make the transition.

A typical reorg is based mainly on head count, job titles, seniority, and possibly age and or high-potential lists. Here the manufacturer used the degree of talent risk and amount of knowledge gaps as chief criteria for evaluating options. The planning process became more data driven—and quickly the picture transformed.

Initially, the director had wanted to organize his new teams by grouping people with a similar expertise in the same physical location. He wanted all his quality-function people to be at the New England plant. He wanted all his scheduling-function people to be at the Midwest plant. He had thought it best if managers were colocated with their teams and the team members were physically together to foster interaction and teamwork. However, there was no money in the budget for physical relocations. His next idea was to find a plant that had a number of quality experts and make that plant the designated quality-function team, retraining others on-site to learn quality systems. He'd find a mass of scheduling or perhaps ordering expertise in a West Coast plant, designate that as the corresponding function team, and reassign all others on-site to that function.

The problem was this scenario resulted in massive talent risk and knowledge transfer demands. See Color Inserts 6 and 7 to view partial KSMs used in scenario planning. When our master consultant on the project, Todd Hudson, reviewed the early scenarios, he told the IT executives that they had too many silos rated "high risk," to which the VP and CIO replied, "Welcome to our world."

"I said, 'Let's look at these ideas. By saying you want all the quality-function people to work at the New England plant, you're taking people who are purple—expert—in scheduling at this location and saying they must become yellow to learn quality, for example. And your people who are purple in quality elsewhere in the world, you want them to become yellow to learn scheduling, ordering, or some other function.'

"The amount of learning people would have to do was immense. With The Steve Trautman Co. tools, we can calculate that down to the hours per person. In this case, it was going to take about four years for them all to learn everything. I said, 'Let's look at the idea of leaving people where they are and consider organizing people into virtual teams around system functions. Let me take all those people and functions and create new KSMs, with less risk and shorter ramp-up times'"

—TODD HUDSON, MASTER CONSULTANT IN
KNOWLEDGE TRANSFER AT THE STEVE TRAUTMAN CO.

The KSM data showed the director where it made sense to break his own rule of colocating workers. He also realized that some people would need to work virtually. The director and his managers mapped out additional scenarios until he found an acceptable risk and knowledge transfer level for his reorg plan.

"There were some quick wins if individuals worked virtually rather than be constrained in the manner of a same physical location. It then became apparent that, OK, this could work. The KSM showed us this. That was really useful."

—THE MANUFACTURER'S DIRECTOR FOR
GLOBAL PLANT SYSTEMS

A Reorg with Realistic Timelines for Risk Reduction

Another benefit of using the KSM to plan the reorganization was it made the multiyear nature of the transition obvious and helped focus annual planning and knowledge transfer efforts. Specifically, once managers and subject matter experts answered approximately how many skills comprised each knowledge silo, the director could use the KSM to predict how long it would take before new teams would be fully up to speed and measurably ready to do their new work.

Clients who use our knowledge transfer process know that any skill can be broken down and taught by an expert to a qualified apprentice in about an hour. So, for example, if a silo in one of the manufacturer's KSMs for a new team has sixty skills in it and three people would need to become "green"—consistent with the expert and able to work independently—in that silo, then the plant systems director knows it will take about 180 hours to transfer the knowledge needed to make the reorg transition for that area of expertise. By adding up all the skills in all the silos that needed to be transferred into new heads and hands, the director could have a total number of hours needed to reduce the talent risk due to knowledge gaps and complete his reorg transition.

As the director and his management team worked through different reorg scenarios using the KSM, they calculated how long each option would reasonably take and used this criterion as a factor in their decision making. Once they had finalized their reorg plans to form five core centralized teams, they then used timing data to set realistic expectations for the transition up and down the organization and set targets for the pace at which knowledge transfer would occur.

> *"What Steve's team helped me do with the KSM was mapping my current state, knowing what my desired end-state was going to be, and then building the plan to get there. I looked at that as a two- or three-year time horizon."*

> —The manufacturer's Director for
> Global Plant Systems

MANAGING TALENT RISK WHEN DOWNSIZING

As the industry downturn worsened, the plant systems support teams were hit by several waves of layoffs. The director had been told each time to "get more costs down." When the reorganization planning had begun, the global plant systems team totaled 160 people. By the time people were moved into their new roles and working independently, the director's staff had been cut to about fifty. The director had to manage his team's talent risk throughout this hefty downsizing—*and* amid a major reorganization *and* while still making sure daily responsibilities were met to keep the wheels on the bus. That's a great deal of risk.

One of the most important actions the director took in the reductions was the unusual (by most companies' standards) step of making the level of talent risk on the KSM as a selection criteria for layoffs. The director knew he had to ensure a minimum level of knowledge in every critical silo, regardless of an employee's performance.

"Of course, I made the decisions of who to put forward for layoff and release. That begged the question, 'How do I decide who to put on that list?' Performance is obviously one factor, but you quickly have no low performers left when you're reducing by what was eventually 60 percent. The low performers were gone a long time ago. That's where the Knowledge Silo Matrices really helped.

"I looked at the question through the lens of, 'OK, I've got various systems I cannot afford to let fail. I must have knowledge of these systems and maintain them. They are business critical. I've got to have a certain weight of knowledge in each.' So I rank all my priorities, all my criticality on the systems, and start to look at asking, 'Which systems am I weak in on personnel? Which have got multiple layers? Where is my knowledge? Who can I afford to release from a business criticality perspective? What is the flight risk of various individuals? . . . And then what is my risk

management plan now based on those layoffs?' That's what I've been doing."

—The manufacturer's Director for
Global Plant Systems

If a mediocre performer in the director's team was the sole purple or green in a knowledge silo, he kept them. In fact, in one case the director kept a lower performer who was also a flight risk because the person exclusively held knowledge for a key silo. The director worked with HR to incentivize this person to stay until they could "extract all the knowledge she had about the silo."

Further, when senior executives or HR staff would question the director's choices—"Why aren't you getting rid of that person instead of this person? Look, we've ranked those who remain and that person is now at the bottom"—the director had a clear, data-driven response.

"I can show HR, 'Well, that person might sit at the bottom of your ladder bank, but let me show you what knowledge they've got that nobody else in the organization has and the impact of getting rid of that knowledge and the risk to our manufacturing if we did.' That's what I presented to my execs when they questioned the plan. That was really, really powerful."

—The manufacturer's Director for
Global Plant Systems

Remarkably, even with these reductions and the stressors to his workforce, the director was able to continue supporting his internal customers. His team continued executing both "break-fix" issues and improvement projects important to moving the reorg along. Also, our process for managing talent risk provided him and his staff a common vocabulary and method to use. It was "a crutch they could all lean on during a very difficult period."

It shouldn't be surprising that I advocate this director's approach as a best management practice. Yes, performance is the universally accepted key criterion for layoffs, and it's easily justified by annual performance reviews. But talent risk and the KSM data are new types of documented criteria and evaluation that should be considered as important in downsizing decisions, as this manufacturer proved. Because talent risk *is* business risk. A failure in a single critical silo can result in a blunder that affects even the stock price.

SPEED OF RESULTS BROKE THROUGH RESISTANCE TO CHANGE

The director's reorg plans had been developed with the help of his management team. The managers helped paint the reorg challenges and potential solutions so they were fully behind the new plan by the time the manufacturer rolled it out. After kickoff, the client held a series of knowledge transfer workshops to train the experts and their apprentices on the best techniques to transfer their heavily technical knowledge.

Workers went into the workshops "with a lot of doubt" about the success of the reorg and the overall plan. The doubt was rooted in a typical resistance to change. Most of the team members were talented individuals who had worked for the manufacturer for twenty- or thirty-plus years. While the loyalty and longevity in the organization was a blessing, it also came with a "this is the way we've always done it" attitude.

> *"I kept saying that this is what we're going to do. We're going to make this move. And these are all the business reasons why. And they kept asking me, 'But how are we going do it, [boss]? We hear*

what you're saying, but how are we going to move from this team to that team?' I kept saying, 'Knowledge transfer. Don't worry, knowledge transfer.'

"I was very delighted that it went the way I'd hoped from a cultural perspective. They came out of each workshop very buoyed up, very positive. They were saying, 'Yeah, we can see how this could work.'"

—THE MANUFACTURER'S DIRECTOR FOR
GLOBAL PLANT SYSTEMS

Then the teams began transferring knowledge and they drastically changed their outlook. Yes, the first workshop had given the team confidence, but seeing the plan working, seeing knowledge being measurably transferred and talent gaps being reduced, and seeing new team members successfully assuming their responsibilities broke down remaining resistance to change.

"I would track what skills we had been transferring in that month and how many applications would move over. People started to see results, and the resistance to change just evaporated. Everybody became bought in."

—THE MANUFACTURER'S DIRECTOR FOR
GLOBAL PLANT SYSTEMS

This story is especially relevant because the i4cp research findings from their 2016 Talent Risk Management survey show that "resistance to change in our culture" is the second-highest barrier to an organization addressing its talent risk; not having a feasible process for analyzing talent risk is top on the list.[25] Here the manufacturer is a great example

---

25 "Preliminary Results: Talent Risk Management Survey," Institute for Corporate Productivity, March 2016.

of overcoming that resistance through accountability to a good talent risk management approach and knowledge transfer process.

SETTING TALENT RISK METRICS FOR A MULTIYEAR TRANSITION

The reorganization was a multiyear project, because even with the best plan there was still so much knowledge to capture and transfer before people could assume their new roles. The director knew his team couldn't do this all at once, nor could they let this work slip. He began by using the KSM to set individual employee knowledge transfer goals.

"We can't feed the elephant in one sitting. We need to chip away at this. It's going to take the next several years. Well, how much time, how much of my capacity do I want my people to commit to this each month or each week? In talking with Steve [Trautman], I decided 10 percent sounds about right. I don't want more than 10 percent because I've still got to deliver. I've still got to support operations. I don't want everybody to go running off all excited and spending 80 percent of their time for six months doing this because my deliveries will suffer.

"Similarly, I don't want people to go off and think, 'Oh, [leadership] isn't committed to this. We don't really need to do it.' To make sure that didn't happen I said I want to see at least 5 percent. I set us up with individual goals between 5 and 10 percent as the expected average capacity utilization each week, each month for knowledge transfer."

—THE MANUFACTURER'S DIRECTOR FOR
GLOBAL PLANT SYSTEMS

When a layoff wave hit, it would complicate this plan, but the targets still proved useful. During the initial layoff period, key people took early retirement. The KSM made their expertise clear, and the Skill Development Plans (SDP) gave them a process to transfer what they knew and not leave out anything important. In one case, this meant two departing experts spent 30 percent of their time during their last months transferring knowledge. In other cases, where the director had intended the 10 percent target, he had to reduce that goal to between 2 percent and 5 percent due to the layoffs. Still, with clear directives, the knowledge transfer and risk reduction continued each month until the new centralized teams took on their new functions.

Another key metric established was department-level yearly goals. The first year's goal was the number of skills transferred each month. The director wanted to get that granular. He also wanted to track the number of people moving from yellow to green (individual talent risk fully mitigated). That "got the momentum going" because everyone could see if they were achieving what they needed to achieve and whether they were ahead of the pack or falling behind. By the second year, the director set a higher-level department metric: the number of silos completed and owned by the right team (progression of the reorg). He ended the first year at 40 percent and the next year at 70 percent. The third year's goal was 100 percent.

"That's my metric for the second year because at the end of the day my overall goal isn't to transfer knowledge—my original goal is to stand up my centralized team . . . My goal is common toolsets and more efficient and quicker delivery to our customers."

—THE MANUFACTURER'S DIRECTOR FOR
GLOBAL PLANT SYSTEMS

CLEAR, MEASURABLE RESULTS

The reorg itself is complete and considered a success. The plant systems team proved that it could maintain their support of plant operations with almost two-thirds fewer people. Success means "work coming in and handled by the right team." This is happening almost 80 percent of the time and is marking toward 100 percent. People aren't just green on their KSM chart, they're "confident in their ability to do the work and meet their responsibilities." The possibility of optimizing the plant systems for greater efficiency is no longer simply a concept, but is now within reach.

The talent risk tools and the common language are now embedded into the IT team's culture and are used daily. The director continues to manage with these facts in creative ways up and down the chain of command.

> *"This gave me a brilliant toolset that I could use for my planning . . . Initially, it was put into planning the reorganization. I then used it for the reductions. Now I'm using it to consolidate the organization, to manage flight risk and for ongoing talent management.*
>
> *"All the organization's departments are still being challenged by our executives: How can you create more cost savings? How can you reorganize to be more effective? Now I've got data to show them in a simplified format that I'm already in the most lean organizational structure I could be in."*
>
> —THE MANUFACTURER'S DIRECTOR FOR
> GLOBAL PLANT SYSTEMS

Finally, the director's current team has weathered the layoffs, and many are now energized to be gaining so much new knowledge. Numerous software engineers who went to university decades ago are coming to the director saying, "I really want to learn these new languages. This is great. This is modern technology." At the same time, management is using their KSMs to target people they need to recruit into the organization.

> *"Where can I best use my recruitment budget to get the maximum return for the corporation? I know that because of my IT roadmap of what systems I want moving forward, I can say, 'Bring on this person with these skill sets. And this is going to cost us that— but here is the return on investment.' My KSMs help me do that investment calculation for recruitment."*
>
> —THE MANUFACTURER'S DIRECTOR FOR
> GLOBAL PLANT SYSTEMS

Outsourcing & Consistency— a Fortune 500 Software Developer

A team of technical writers working for a multinational software developer creates software documentation such as help files, user guides, and error messages for the company's products. Half of the technical writing team is spread across the United States, and the other half is in India. The time difference across the geographies allows the team to deliver content on demand 24/7.

CHALLENGES:

- Consistency across global and culturally diverse teams
- Load leveling issues
- Too much rework
- Skill shortages
- Consistent training without high financial and opportunity costs
- Relevant, real-time, and on-the-job guidance

THE BUSINESS PROBLEM

The benefits of on-demand assistance came with a price. The writing team struggled with consistency—everything from research methods to critical areas such as developer relations, project estimation, and document design. Having no established standards combined with the team's approach of creating a new document for each new request meant there was a high degree of time-consuming and expensive— and probably unnecessary—rework. The team's struggle with being nimble enough to shift work between writers with the necessary skill sets added to these problems.

Company leadership asked the team to use a new writing model called "structured authoring." The model is designed to increase productivity and decrease rework by putting consistent standards in place that could be duplicated across teams anywhere in the world.

The organization put the authoring system in place and set up classroom training sessions in key locations. It looked like all systems were go, and expectations of success were high.

THE KEY CHALLENGES

Traditional classroom training is the go-to method for getting people up to speed on new skills and procedures. Typically, employees sit down together for a one-size-fits-all class at some point in time. For this organization, the skill levels on the writing team varied widely. The advanced participants felt it was a waste of their time to listen to basic skill training that they could probably perform in their sleep. The lesser-skilled workers were overwhelmed. They furiously scribbled notes but usually had no idea how to differentiate the information into "need to know," "good to know," and "so obscure you will maybe see this twice in your career" rankings. The one-size-fits-all approach also meant that regardless of their skill and knowledge level, team members would need to sift through training materials that covered *all* jobs to find material specific to *their* job. Plus, team members were unlikely to implement what they'd learned until a week or even a month later. At that point, most of them would have forgotten what they'd learned.

The training challenge was to slice and dice the information so it would be easy to find and learn, regardless of time zone or location. The one-size-fits-all material had to be replaced with targeted skill-training material relevant to each team member. We wanted the company to be able to train the entire current team—and future teams—without flying experts halfway around the world for weeks at a time.

KNOWLEDGE AND SKILLS REVEAL THE RISKS

The KSM quickly revealed that a large number of silos had a preponderance of yellow "Actively Learning" members, and a few silos had an overabundance of green "Able to Work Independently" members. This might have been OK if the majority of silos hadn't lacked an expert to set the standard. It was no wonder the team had a major consistency issue. More troubling was the issue that seven of the thirty-three silos were marked red—high risk. It became obvious that the team lacked sufficient bench strength to implement and sustain the new writing approach. See Color Insert 8.

I want to point out a rookie mistake that some managers and teams make when they first get their hands on the matrix. Without clear communication and process discipline, some first-time participants go overboard on skills and silos, overdoing the knowledge transfer process, costing the project speed and manageability.

A manager based in India ended up pushing back the project timeline when her team decided they wanted more granular information for each silo. A knowledge silo generally represents twenty to one hundred job skills. The team had taken each silo and added two or three sub-silos. Each new sub-silo then had up to five different skills in them. Given our two decades of knowledge transfer experience, we immediately knew that the knowledge areas were now broken down *too much,* and any resulting transfer process would likely be too cumbersome. Lesson learned: Stick to the methodology and resist urges to make the process more detailed and complicated than necessary.

REDUCING THE RISK

Using the data from the KSM, the team developed Skill Development Plans (SDPs) for each at-risk silo of the team. It quickly became evident that the company's top priority should be to develop a complete set of mentors in India (one for each silo) who were consistent with their counterpart mentors in the US (one for each silo).

When Mentors Are in Short Supply

The team had just a few stateside employees who qualified as mentors (purple). They would shoulder the brunt of the standard-bearing work in a large number of knowledge silos. The talent risk was high, and the speed of risk reduction was vital. But running individual knowledge transfer sessions with many apprentices (yellow) concurrently would overload and potentially burn out the few silo mentors the developer had.

In addition, a new hire joined the technical writing team in a critical position soon after the knowledge transfer project began. This hire had to learn a lot of skills across many silos. The mentor for each of these silos was already at full capacity, and management couldn't wait for the designated mentor-in-training to complete their learning and become an active mentor. So the developer used a "skill mentor."

A "**skill mentor**" is an employee who has not yet learned *all* the skills needed on their customized SDP, but has mastered a *given* skill, passed their mentor's test questions in full for that skill, and has typically begun using the skill on the job. This approach starts to level the workload of busy mentors by pushing certain mentoring responsibilities down deeper into the team's bench strength, allowing a greater number of apprentices to be trained at one time. It also rewards the advancing employee because he or she doesn't have to wait long to try their hand at mentoring.

The developer also used group mentoring. "**Group mentoring**" is when a silo mentor has multiple apprentices who have more or less the same skill sets to build on, and—for the sake of expediency and load leveling—the mentor will work with these apprentices at the same time. Two or three apprentices will sync up their training session dates and their target completion dates per skill, so the mentor is able to focus on a given skill and run the skill's knowledge transfer session for these apprentices at the same time. However, each apprentice must take their skill test separately.

Employees Still Need to Get Work Done

Obviously, work can't stop while everyone gets up to speed. The project's knowledge transfer process owner set a group target that employees would spend 10 percent of their time each week on knowledge transfer and 90 percent on their regular work. This clarified where knowledge transfer to mitigate talent risk ranked in priority to their weekly work. Apprentices and mentors could move their personal target if they and their manager agreed circumstances warranted the change. The combination of clarity and empowerment helped participants to feel committed and led to more consistent progress. Knowledge transfer responsibilities were also tied to functional job roles (for mentors) and developmental goals (for apprentices)—meaning knowledge transfer completion became included in an employee's bonus plan.

The company's knowledge transfer process owner tracked progress by monitoring two dates on the SDP: the date the apprentice was targeting to complete their knowledge acquisition in a silo, and the actual date of completion. The process owner could see which employees were scheduled to change status in which month (e.g., moving from "apprentice" status to "independent worker" status or, in a few cases, from "independent worker" status to "mentor" status). She could then *predict* when she would have a new mentor in a given silo to alleviate the workload on the few mentors who initially started the project. Over time, she could see if any groups or a certain manager's reports were *failing* to progress. Since apprentices were updating their customized SDPs regularly, tracking was easy because the process owner simply had to review individual SDPs in a shared folder.

Unexpected Changes

A change in internal leadership during the process does not spell disaster for a knowledge transfer project. The direct manager position for the team was open when the project began. About two months into the knowledge transfer timeline, the position was filled by a longtime manager at the company. While an accomplished manager, she had no technical writing experience and no familiarity with knowledge transfer.

She used the team's Knowledge Silo Matrix, Skill Development Plans, and Communication and Change Management Planner to quickly figure out a large part of her job. She became a student of her team's work and was able to learn a lot about their roles and situation in a short time.

These types of changes happen all the time. The data and planning developed to manage talent risk reduce the impact of major changes. The tools help managers to better understand and lead their teams overall. And, the tools are great ready-made orientation documents for new hires.

CLEAR, MEASURABLE RESULTS

At the beginning of the project, the organization faced problems typical of any company with geographically (and culturally) diverse teams—getting and keeping teams working to the same standards regardless of location.

The team in India had no team members who had the knowledge and skills to be on-location standard bearers for the new, right way to do things. In this instance, the US-based team had a bit of this going on too. Within its first two quarters of completing their talent risk assessment, *the software developer confidently upgraded five Indian workers to stan-dard-bearing expert status*—each consistent in every skill with their US counterparts—mitigating the company's talent risks in its most critical knowledge silos. In addition, the team can now catch and avoid poten-tial inconsistencies, reducing instances of rework. More importantly, the team is completing more work with fewer writers. (See Table 3.)

TEAM PRODUCTIVITY PRE- AND POST-KNOWLEDGE TRANSFER TRAINING	
Q4 2011	Q4 2012
53 active programs	57 active programs
10 significant software releases	21 significant software releases
36 writers	31 writers
	PLUS: able to take on special initiatives (SA, resource management, video, etc.)

Table 3. Productivity measurements Q4 2011 to Q4 2012. The team completed 8% more projects with 14% fewer writers.

By having two experts consistent with each other—one in the US and one in India—for every knowledge silo of their multinational writing team, the developer has increased not only the speed but also the volume of people they can onboard in either nation. Much like the employees who quickly went from proficient to expert within two quarters, thirteen team members went from apprentice status to working independently on the job. After another two quarters, the developer predicts seventy-five team members will shift up in silo skill level. New team members are getting up to speed, further increasing the productivity of the team.

> *"Now that we're using knowledge transfer, if somebody asks, 'What's the average time required for someone to move from not knowing to being able to use a skill on the job?' I can do some easy math and give it to them. That makes us both better managers."*
>
> —THE KNOWLEDGE TRANSFER PROCESS OWNER

A master SDP for the company's technical writing job role now stands as both a skill set that informs future hiring and a ready-made orientation plan, saving time and money. This tool can also identify new hires or reassignments who are lagging behind the normal learning time for a certain knowledge silo, giving early detection to potential capability problems or a bad hire.

The Future State of Talent Risk Management

FOR OVER TWENTY YEARS, MY TEAM AND I HAVE BEEN WORKING ON the concept of knowledge transfer and talent risk management. We've seen multiple wholesale changes in how we think and act as business leaders, particularly as we've learned more about managing a global and increasingly complex workforce. Insourcing, outsourcing, off-shoring, job sharing, crowd sourcing, and the gig economy are buzz-words on a continuum of staid to radical. Getting the day-to-day work done on time, on budget, and with a high degree of consistency and quality has never been more challenging as we navigate from "tried and true" to "holy cow, we're doing what!?"

In the introduction of this book, I said that I once heard the chief risk officer for a major international insurance company describe the president of her region as the "chief risk taker." I said that if you think of chief risk taker, you might picture a daredevil dressed like Elvis preparing to ride his motorcycle up a ramp and over a row of buses. Well, in this chapter, I want to paint a picture of how organizations can make sure Elvis lands safely on the other side.

The ideas put forth in this book have been in place and making a difference for years. In the age of big data, we've shown that more data isn't better (no matter how beautifully presented) if it isn't fundamentally able to help improve quality, speed, and profitability.

> " In the age of big data, we've shown that more data isn't better (no matter how beautifully presented) if it isn't fundamentally able to help improve quality, speed, and profitability."

"Garbage in, garbage out," as they say. Instead, it is imperative that business leaders not settle for anything less than data that directly answers the question, "Will I have enough workers with the right technical skills to execute my business strategy three to thirty-six months from now?"

At each level of leadership, executives to frontline leaders are already managing their talent risk in substantially new and valuable ways. What follows is a summary of how that looks in practice.

TALENT RISK MANAGEMENT TOP TO BOTTOM

I hope I've made the case that if you want a dependably competitive workforce, you *cannot* get one without managing your talent risks as an integral part of managing every change. The way forward is discussed a little differently at every level of leadership, but the talent risk component can be a common thread that ties it all together. Corporate boards will discuss transitions like replacing the CEO or approving new corporate strategies. C-level executives will discuss transitions like mergers and acquisitions, new competitive threats, opening new markets, and investing in new technologies. Mid-level leaders will discuss transitions like growth, reorganizing, outsourcing, and right-sizing. Frontline employees and their managers will discuss transitions that directly affect their everyday tasks like being assigned to a new project or rolling out a new technology. All of these leaders can be aligned in responding to and staffing those transitions using the common framework and lexicon from this book.

Without a talent risk mitigation plan, these changes risk the underuse, burnout, or even loss of your best talent. No high-performing organization should settle for that. As you read through this section, you can begin to shape your own path forward as a leader but also look for ways to influence both below and above your place in the hierarchy.

Board Level

Corporate boards have a fiduciary responsibility to shareholders, and that is why managing talent risk must be front and center—the stock price depends on it. The National Association of Corporate Directors wrote a Blue Ribbon Commission[26] report on the topic, and they were so clear in their recommendations that I've included them again here in this section unedited. In short, corporate boards need to make talent risk a part of the culture and fabric of the companies they serve.

- To meet future challenges, successful organizations establish multiyear, multilevel internal pipelines of talent. It is vital that the board recognizes that talent, strategy, and risk are inexorably linked.

- Oversight of the company's talent development efforts should be a full board responsibility, with the actual planning and execution owned by management. The standing board committees can oversee the talent development associated with their respective areas of oversight.

- The full board should view human capital through the lens of strategy and risk, with committees providing input to the board on talent development in their respective areas as appropriate. In addition to reviewing the talent factor related

---

26 "BRC Talent Development: A Boardroom Imperative," The National Association of Corporate Directors, 2013.

to every strategic initiative, the board agenda should allocate time—at least annually—to take a deep dive into human capital development.

- Corporate directors should request that management provide a talent component in every strategic initiative presented to the board. Just as an institution is built on the flow of talent upward and across the organization, oversight can be viewed as cascading downward. The talent discussion must be ongoing and supported by a variety of metrics.

Senior Executive Level

Senior executives set strategy and then need to monitor whether that strategy is going to be executed as planned. Once the strategy has been stated, senior execs can and should use talent risk data to earn the trust and manage expectations with their board. Simultaneously, they should use the same data to ensure leaders in their organizations are moving forward efficiently and that any surprises are uncovered and managed well before they impact schedules and budgets.

- Executives must be addicted to making decisions informed by substantive talent risk data and never settle for less than a clear picture of their risk profile.
  - A few hours a month are dedicated to ensuring talent risk data is updated so that even unplanned changes such as needing to respond to an emergent competitive threat can be well informed.
  - Leadership teams and managers will regularly discuss and plan to mitigate talent risk.
  - Reorganizations, mergers, acquisitions, and new site standups will always include scenario planning that is

based on current state talent risks and assesses likely changes to the talent risk profile *before* expensive, complicated, and time-consuming problems crop up.

- ○ No one will consider adding head count or budget for contractors without first ensuring both that existing resources are fully utilized and that new resources are directly tied to reducing the highest talent risk and priorities.

- Since talent expenses routinely top 50 percent of total corporate spend, executives will develop budgets that *spend money to monitor and manage the risks* associated with that investment.

- There will be increasing demand for organizations to be nimbler so they can respond to global and local changes faster. That means it can't take months or years to pivot from the old way to the new way during a big change.

- For many highly technical roles, the notion of full employment is coming soon and will further exacerbate the need to maximize the talent you have. Other approaches that you've settled for in the past won't get you there; you will need data-driven talent risk management.

- Responding to the global need for consistency while keeping room for autonomy and creativity is a pendulum. It is the push and pull of control versus freedom. By identifying the "purple," you eliminate ambiguity in the process—which leaves people more time to be creative.

- Cries for culture or systemic change will continue to be an elusive siren song until organizations can figure out "who's purple" for the change. If you can't identify the "purple for culture," you don't really know what you want, and your people won't know either.

- New ideas for how technology will be a driver/enabler for skill development will continue to surface, but at the end of the day two questions must always be answered before any technology can be fully useful: Who is purple and who is yellow? Those simple questions aren't answered by technology, and no amount of technology will make up for the lack of answers.

Middle Management Level

Leaders—directors and vice presidents leading groups of fifty to five hundred people—in the middle of the organizational structure are the true heroes of any organization. They have to take the sometimes unclear vision and strategy from above and make it doable below. They must figure out what is possible and say no to what is not. They have to solve enterprise problems with an eye toward the individuals who end up making the difference between winning and losing. These are the people who will be digging into the data—living it and breathing it. They are the chess masters, and the KSMs are the chess boards.

- Enterprise leaders will be expected to measure that they've made a solid connection between the strategy set by their C-level bosses and the actions taken by their frontline teams.

- These leaders will monitor alignment on talent issues between the various teams in their organization as a measure of health. They will no longer settle for gut feel guiding a status report on alignment.

- These leaders will use talent risk data to "manage up" when it comes to setting expectations on what can be accomplished and by when. The information provided by these leaders will be used by executives to manage expectations with the board and even with Wall Street.

- Increasingly, budgets are not controlled by this layer of management as in the past, and middle managers will become more adept at influencing budget decisions to invest in mitigating talent risk. They'll use "cost of a mistake data" to make it harder to cut talent budgets without first carefully considering the implications.

- Outsource partners will be managed with talent risk data as a foundation for contract negotiations, service level feedback, and to ensure they meet quality standards.

- The KSM will supplant competency models as the next-gen talent management practice of choice for all technical roles.

- They'll insist that data from human capital analytics includes both macro reporting across the enterprise and micro reporting about unique people working in their organization.

Frontline Leaders and Staff

Frontline workers and their leaders are where the rubber hits the road for talent risk management. Nothing about talent risk is academic for the people who get up every day and deliver the products and services that underpin corporate profits. For them, it affects quality, productivity, time recovering from change, frustration levels, and how often they get home to dinner with their families. Most workers want simply to know what is expected and to deliver on that consistently, and talent risk data must be used to monitor and manage that every day.

- Employees and contractors will "learn how to learn" to drive talent risk mitigation from the bottom up. This includes answering three questions as a matter of course: How do I fit in the Big Picture? What are my tasks? How do I know if I'm doing them right?

- Onboarding time will be cut by 50 percent for new hires, contractors, partners, and internal transfers.

- Experts and "standard-setters" will be identified and will routinely transfer knowledge at a set number of hours per week (management sets the target time).

- Employees will drive their own customized SDPs to close knowledge gaps, ensure consistency, and further their careers.

- When confronted with an organizational change, the leader will say, "Which silos am I losing or picking up? Which people am I losing or picking up? OK, I'll let you know how that affects my team's risk profile by tomorrow and then I'll tell you what we're going to do about it by the end of the week."

- Every employee will have a known and developing technical skill set so they can be deployed to highest advantage.

- Employees will have tools, processes, and support from management to maintain knowledge transfer over the long term.

Human Resources, Talent Management, Learning Professionals

For the last three decades or more, human capital professionals have worked to get a seat at the table as true business partners with the line executives they serve. I have seen this evolution firsthand since I ran learning at Microsoft and, more recently, because my firm's clients are mostly business leaders who may or may not invite their HR partners to the table. In the ongoing quest to be more relevant and look for the next big thing, strategic workforce planning is waning and the idea of human capital analytics is on the upswing. Human capital professionals must not be seduced by the idea that big data and HCA are going to make a real difference to the business in their current form.

If the data doesn't allow you to zoom in on the unique individuals who directly impact revenue, quality, and speed, it doesn't matter to your business partners. Don't settle for giving them any less than that.

> " Human capital professionals must not be seduced by the idea that big data and HCA are going to make a real difference to the business in their current form."

- Talent risk data will be gathered, maintained, and put front and center, influencing every business decision; human capital professionals will become fluent in their businesses because they are fluent in the data.

- HCA efforts will be augmented to provide talent risk reports that directly point to revenue, quality, and speed—the key drivers that every business leader needs to influence most.

- CHROs will monitor and respond to trends in available technical talent in a more granular way with the KSM as the backdrop.

- CHROs and line-of-business leaders will advocate for budgets that pay for talent risk management methodology and processes as a business imperative.

- The KSM will augment or supplant competency models as the next-gen talent management practice of choice for all technical roles.

- When competing for top-tier talent, interviews will include the KSM as a backdrop for the types of well-organized development opportunities an employee could expect if he or she accepted an offer.

- Performance reviews for leaders will include a look at how they are tracking and mitigating talent risk for the employees and contractors on their teams.

Don't Settle

I want to leave you with confidence that, while this list may appear utopian, it is real and already in practice at major companies around the world. The effort is still in its early days, but no part of this is unproven. So I want you to consider: What steps can you take to make this happen in your organization?

As you've been reading along, I'm sure that many times you thought that the ideas I've presented are pretty good but not something you haven't already seen. Or maybe they seem so straightforward that you might imagine them to be familiar, and that familiarity is comfortable so you bopped along through the book, pleased with yourself for already being on top of much of this. Or it could be that you read the book and found a twist that was interesting and you thought, "Well now, that's something to think about. I should try this point," but that is as far as you've gone. All these sentiments are the loud screaming voice of inertia masquerading as a whisper in your ear. It is telling you to nod knowingly and then step away from the book that might cause you to act.

So, here's my charge. No matter your level of leadership or span of control, you can begin talking about the idea of talent risk. You can start asking for and collecting talent risk data that lives at the intersection of strategy, people, and risk. You can challenge yourself to be sure these three things are true for you and for anyone who works for you.

1. Strategy: I know I understand the strategy because I can explain it in plain language to my boss and my peers, and we all sound alike. I get the Big Picture.

2. People: I can describe the unique technical skills required to execute the strategy, and I either know the names of the actual people who will execute it or I can say where I am going to find them.

3. Risk: I have data to quantify the risks of not being able to execute the strategy due to people issues, and I have a plan to mitigate that risk.

Don't settle for anything less.

Start Your Talent Risk Management Transformation in the Next 90 Minutes

IN ORGANIZATIONAL TRANSITIONS, SUCH AS ACQUISITIONS, REORGA-nizations, project startups, new hires, and retirements, there are "people who know" and "people who need to know." To be proactive in the face of these transitions, managers must assess the skills and knowledge needed for the future, analyze the talent pool they already have, document the gap, and create a plan to bridge it—reducing risk along the way. All this must happen quickly and on top of an already busy schedule.

Start your own TRM transformation with our sample Knowledge Silo Matrix (see Resources at www.stevetrautman.com). This framework will help you—

- Count the individuals who have the expertise and who can do the work associated with a specific knowledge domain, or "silo."

- Note the individuals who would be appropriate to train others, because they are not only capable of doing the work, but their *approach* sets the standards for others.

- Call out individuals who need to learn specific silos or who need to be more consistent with the mentor.

- Highlight current and potential risks to the team's ability to get the job done.

If you are a manager of a team with up to ten employees and/or contractors, you can create a Knowledge Silo Matrix (KSM) for them in about ninety minutes.[27]

Enter the names of the Knowledge Silos for your team or department. Remember, a silo is a group of skills and tasks (typically twenty to one hundred) that represent a block of work within a team. Silos can be technical expertise, tools, processes, products, standards, customers, and physical locations. The sample KSM has room for ten silos, but your team may have many more.

In the Employee/Contractor column, you can enter the names of the people you want to include in the exercise. Be sure to include individuals who are borrowed from other teams and those who work for you only episodically. You want to document the entire "ecosystem" of talent required to get the work done for your team. For each silo, you should indicate if the person is the standard-bearer (purple), independently working (green), actively learning (yellow), or not using the skill (white).

Once you have completed the matrix, look it over. Where are your areas of risk? What are your highest priorities? How do you want to mitigate the risk?

Think about the "cost of a mistake" for your risks. You can run through various scenarios to model the costs using our Cost of a Mistake Calculator, also found in the website resources at www.steve trautman.com. Other tools on the website help you explore how to use knowledge transfer to mitigate risk.

---

27 If you lead a larger organization, you'll find that the data in the matrix will quickly become inconsistent and less useful unless you have proper tools and training to implement a KSMx. You can learn more about the KSMx at www.stevetrautman.com.

About the Research

THE TALENT RISK RESEARCH BY THE NONPROFIT INSTITUTE OF Corporate Productivity (i4cp) quoted throughout this book was conducted in spring of 2016. You can find the research report, "Talent Risk Management," on their website, www.i4cp.com.

The research surveyed executives and senior managers from companies across a broad span of industries, with 60 percent being multinational or global organizations. The majority of companies were headquartered in the US and were large organizations, with two-thirds having 1,000 or more employees. Although some participated from government and nonprofit sectors, nearly 80 percent of respondents were from private or publicly traded corporations. The respondents spanned a range of departments, including CEO/Executive, Operations, Technology/Information, Finance/Accounting, Human Resources, and others. In total, more than 400 respondents took the survey.

After the online questionnaire, i4cp conducted a handful of in-depth qualitative interviews with senior executives at major corporations to get at more detail and yield the short case studies featured in the published report.

The Steve Trautman Co. was one of the organizations privy to the raw data results from the survey and to an initial i4cp findings document not included in the public report. Some of the data points and findings quoted in this book are taken from these raw results.

The research findings highly validate the ideas in this book. For example, independent analysis of the data and interviews by i4cp researchers led the researchers to identify in their report a "next-gen" process for better talent risk management. That process is nearly identical to the process advocated in this book and used by The Steve Trautman Co. for several years prior to the research. The steps of our process vary only in terminology and in the final sustainment step, which we include in all our client work, though it is not named in our formal three-step talent risk management process. Similarly, i4cp's independently derived checklist of twelve best practices published in the report align remarkably with the practical ideas, processes, tools, and advice presented here.

ABOUT THE AUTHOR

IF YOU ARE LOOKING FOR BETTER WAYS TO MANAGE YOUR talent risk, Steve Trautman is *the* talent risk management expert. He initially pioneered the field of technical knowledge transfer, developing the nationally recognized gold standard used by blue-chip companies around the globe. Building on that foundation, Steve brought his practical, data-driven ideas to talent risk management, creating tools that are straightforward and relevant for even the most complex organizations. For more than twenty years, Steve and his team at The Steve Trautman Co. have been providing Fortune 500 executives with the simplest, quickest, and most practical solutions for managing their talent risk, especially in highly technical and professionally skilled teams.

Steve began solving talent-related business problems in 1990 when he developed his first knowledge transfer program (then called "Peer Mentoring") as a young project manager working on Word 1.0 at Microsoft. He developed the program as a response to the intense on-the-job training needs of his rapidly growing technical team. He wanted to help the technical experts around him learn how to be teachers so they could quickly ramp up all the new employees Microsoft was hiring. By 1993, he had cofounded a department at Microsoft to provide training and knowledge transfer for all its employees shipping software worldwide. He later left to form his own company and began rolling out knowledge transfer tools and consulting to businesses across a broad range of industries.

Steve has lived on both sides of the talent management problem and has walked in the shoes of a corporate executive.

He has been both a talent manager and a line executive. In 2000, Expedia.com asked Steve to become general manager of their advertising unit—then a $20 million business—which Steve ran until his growing consulting company required him to return full time.

Over the years, Steve has demonstrated an uncanny gift for clearly defining business problems and explaining them in the plainest language. The ability to assess and mitigate talent risk on an ongoing basis has emerged as a key priority because the existing solutions were so cumbersome. His clients were struggling to find answers that made sense as much on the front line as they did in the C-suite. Steve developed new tools and processes so organizations can easily get at more relevant talent data, talk about their talent risk in a common language, and align on priorities—enterprise wide. Providing measurable returns is paramount in every system Steve designs.

And he continues to innovate. He has written two other books, *Teach What You Know: A Practical Leader's Guide to Knowledge Transfer through Peer Mentoring* (Prentice Hall, 2006) and *The Executive Guide to High-Impact Talent Management* (McGraw Hill, 2011). Steve speaks internationally and provides business leaders with commonsense guidance and support. He is known for his high-energy style that combines humor, street smarts, and boardroom wisdom with terminology and concepts that can be explained in minutes and implemented within hours.

7/17